GH01032699

DONKEYS

DONKEYS

A PRACTICAL GUIDE TO THEIR MANAGEMENT

by

M. R. DE WESSELOW

With drawings by the author

CENTAUR PRESS LTD.

© CENTAUR PRESS LTD., 1967, 1969
Revised edition 1969
New Edition 1973

SBN/900000 01 5

First published 1967 *by the*
Centaur Press Ltd., Fontwell, Sussex
& 11-14 Stanhope Mews West, London, S.W.7.
Printed in Great Britain

CONTENTS

CONTENTS

LIST OF PLATES

ACKNOWLEDGEMENTS

I would like to acknowledge my debt to Mr. F. E. Hunter, M.R.C.V.S., who has given much kind advice not only in our stud work but also in reading over the medical portions of this book.

I would also like to thank Mrs. M. F. Faulkner, to whom I owe my knowledge of trap and harness; Mr. Shuhei Iwamoto, who took many beautiful photographs, some of which are used as illustrations; and lastly my husband, without whose help this book would not have been written.

The Preface was written by my mother, who also provided the necessary stimulus for my task and time in which to undertake it.

THE DONKEY SHOW SOCIETY

Readers may be interested to know of the recently formed Donkey Show Society, which has the aim of promoting and improving the breed and will in time compile a Stud Book. It welcomes as a member anyone who owns or is interested in donkeys. With the encouragement of the Society, Donkey Classes are now in great demand at Horse and Agricultural Shows up and down the country.

The President of the Society is Mr. R. S. Summerhays, a late President of the Arab Horse Society and a knowledgeable writer about horses.

The Secretary is Mrs. Walter Greenway and at present the office is at her house, Picketts Hill Cottage, Headley, Nr. Bordon, Hants.

June 1967
M. R. de W.

Preface

The donkey has got himself into the world of poetry, epic and history, an honour he shares with only a few other animals. The horse, of course, is there by right; and so is the dog. Cows are on the verge of it (one jumped over the moon). Cats, at least the domestic ones, have not been voted in though they turn up sometimes. Tigers and lions are old members. Pigs have an entry though without much flourish attached to it. Burns introduced a mouse. Several species of insect have made the grade.

One wonders what is the passport to this exclusive world. The donkey voice is not at all sweet, nor thrilling, nor even nicely complaining. It is a kind of mechanical groan; a clowning noise, as if all the wrong stops had been pulled out and pushed in careless of the effect produced. One might think that this curious protest of his would disqualify him, but one would be wrong; vocal or silent, wild or tame, his place is secure. He likes clean water to drink but munches contentedly at any snatch of twig found by the wayside. He has often a preoccupied air, as if he had a great deal to think about and was not entirely dependent on his surroundings for well-being. One sees an absent-minded donkey wandering into poetry-land without noticing where he was going, and being welcomed at once as part of the scene. He is humble,

patient and hard-working; does not go much by
rules, but is friendly and holds no grudges. There
is nothing lofty about him although he has his
own dignity. Children, who are usually natural
inhabitants of poetry country, fall for him at sight,
and they rarely grow so old that they cease to love
him.

This book introduces the reader to the donkey
and his ways, and may help him to form his own
conclusions.

M.G.

CHAPTER ONE

Thinking about it

THIS handbook is designed to help those who either know nothing at all or very little about keeping a donkey. In view of the popularity of this animal, deriving in the main from his gentle nature and the particular appeal he seems to make to children, it is important to stress at the beginning that although his material wants may be few and simple, they must be observed — otherwise your pet will surely end up by looking like something that needs to be rescued. As with any other animal, once you have taken charge, he is your responsibility; and it is no good buying a donkey as a gimmick and more or less forgetting about him after a week or two. If you lack the facilities to accommodate and care for a small pony, then you have no justification for feeling you can keep a donkey: his basic needs are just the same. Take this into consideration before you buy your pet and not afterwards.

It is sometimes thought that as donkeys often appear to exist on extremely scanty nourishment in the Mediterranean countries or in almost desert regions, a very small paddock should be sufficient for their needs in England. This ought to be no argument at all. Furthermore, a small paddock intensively grazed and lived in all the year round becomes thoroughly unhealthy for reasons shown later in this book, whereas the barren hillsides cropped by the donkey in other countries give endless change of pasture although it may be scanty, and consequently they don't harbour the same parasites. Also, it should be borne in mind that for two or three months of the year most of the warmer countries have lush vegetation, and all the grass-eating animals use every opportunity during this time to eat as much as they can, thus undoubtedly storing a reserve of strength to draw upon in leaner times.

So far this introduction may sound discouraging because it is necessary to face the disadvantages in a general way before thinking further of buying. I certainly have no wish to discourage anyone who has the facilities from owning a donkey, as he makes the most lovable pet and is especially valuable in giving confidence to children who are nervous of larger animals; but I do not like to see him exploited by those who find it amusing to own him but are careless and ignorant about his well-being. I must add one last warning in the same vein. Some of those who have come to us to buy donkeys, tell us earnestly that the animal in question is to be a pet for their children and will be entirely in those children's charge. This attitude shows as much ignorance of children as of animals: no young child can possibly be made responsible for any animal's welfare without adult supervision. A pet may be beloved, but that is quite a different matter from seeing to its daily needs. Of course children vary as to the age at which they become conscientious about these things, but most of them have not the painstaking ability to remember, and execute without prompting, the necessary daily care — however little this may be — connected with looking after a pet.

Although in this country the donkey falls into the categories of pet, grass-controller and companion for horses, undoubtedly his main role is with children. A well-trained and quiet donkey is ideal for very small children and also for nervous ones; there is such a short distance to fall to the ground from his back, and if someone does fall off, the donkey stays put and waits for the next go. His hair being long and soft gives an extra feeling of security to small hands and, unless trained to go fast, his pace is naturally steady and slow. Last but not least, he has a kindly and reassuring eye. I don't think I have ever met a child who was afraid of a donkey.

His great characteristic is sociability. He loves attention from humans and seems to have a particular fondness for children. It is unkind to leave him to himself without either plenty of human company or else an animal companion. If he hasn't the one, he will want the other, and deprived of both he will almost certainly show his loneliness by braying. If you are away from home a good deal and if you have the space, why not think in terms of two donkeys? Failing this, however, he will make friends with something as different as a sheep. Even a duck or goose might provide some sort of companionship — in fact any creature within reason that is kept in the same enclosure will be better than nothing at all.

Finally, while on the topic of welfare, when you go away on holiday, be sure to ask someone to come and visit your donkey every day. Accidents can and do happen, especially when an animal is lonely, and are nearly always unforeseen; a daily check that all is well is a real necessity.

CHAPTER TWO

Buying a donkey

ONCE you have made up your mind to buy a donkey you may have no idea how you go about finding one. There are several people who breed them in this country and the best way of getting in touch with a stud is to write to the Secretary of the Donkey Show Society (page 10). Otherwise follow the Livestock column of your local paper or go to a horsefair.

Once you have located a donkey source, there arises the question of whether to buy a mare (usually known as a Jenny), a gelding, or a stallion (also known as a Jack Ass); a large one or a small one; old or young; and even what colour. The

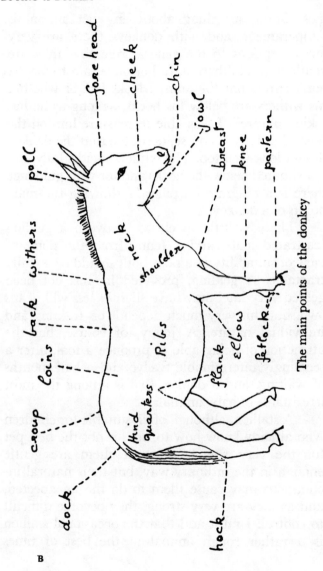

The main points of the donkey

poll
withers
back
loins
croup
dock
neck
shoulder
Ribs
Hind quarters
flank
elbow
fetlock
hock
forehead
cheek
chin
jowl
breast
knee
pastern

B

most important thing about any pet animal is temperament, and with donkeys there are very few exceptions to the general rule that they are gentle with children. A father once said to me, "I don't care what the animal looks like or whether his withers are below his hocks, as long as he has a kind nature". I was able to reassure him on the point, but it is, of course, desirable that the donkey should look well too. The withers incidentally, are not situated below the hocks and for your guidance there is a diagram on page 17 showing the main points of a donkey.

There is little to choose between a gelding (castrated male) and a Jenny from the point of view of suitability as a pet: both should be equally tractable. A gelding, provided he has not been gelded very late, may have slightly less will of his own, but this very much depends on training and individual nature. A Jenny, of course, has the attraction of being able to produce a foal, after a seemingly interminable twelve and a half months of waiting, and a donkey foal is among the most irresistable of baby animals.

A stallion, although often suitable for children who already know how to ride, is not the best pet for the very young. Most of them are gentle enough in the ordinary way, but their natural inclinations may cause them to do the unexpected, and as they are very strong, they become difficult to control. I must add that the occasional stallion is a rather rough animal at the best of times although we have not so far been personally acquainted with one. Probably the sloppiest donkey we have ever owned was a stallion — KoKo by name. He was tall, standing just under twelve hands, and he loved to lean against you with half-shut eyes while you tickled him behind the ears! For older children, I would go so far as to say that the right stallion could be more fun than the more spiritless geldings. He can 'go' all right and be very affectionate, *but* you can't keep him on his own. He must have one or more Jennies for company. Otherwise he will almost certainly become vicious or even savage and probably break out in order to search for a mate. The mate may turn out to be a neighbour's pony mare in which case you will not be very popular.

If you want to have two donkeys, then you can keep any combination of Jennies, foals or geldings together, but don't keep a stallion and a gelding unless they have been brought up together, as the former will usually bully the gelding, who is no match for him. And don't keep two stallions; again, if they have been brought up together, they may get on all right as long as they are kept away from mares — but once they get wind of a Jenny, or even a pony mare, then you are in for trouble, as they will certainly fight.

So much for the sex of the donkey. The next thing that most people worry about is age. You tell a donkey's age by his teeth in the same way as you do a horse's, and although this isn't very hard

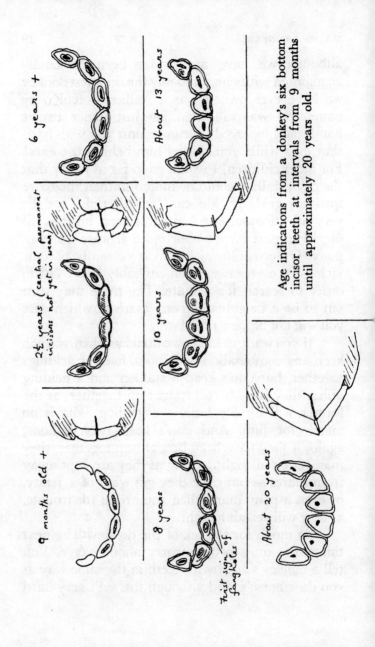

6 years +

About 13 years

2½ years (central permanent incisors not yet in wear)

10 years

9 months old +

First sign of Tangtales

8 years

About 20 years

Age indications from a donkey's six bottom incisor teeth at intervals from 9 months until approximately 20 years old.

to do, you have first to be initiated into the secret of doing it. You go by the teeth of the bottom jaw, as they are easier to see, and the clue to the age lies in the grooves or marks on top of the teeth. The hardest thing to tell sometimes is the difference between the milk teeth and the permanent teeth, as the marks are there in both and the difference only lies in the colour and shape of the teeth themselves: the milk teeth are smaller and whiter, but only experience will make this plain. The key teeth are the six front ones, known as incisors. He loses the two central milk teeth first at the age of two and a half years, the next two (the laterals) when he is three and a half and at four and a half he loses the two "corners". Although he will then have his six permanent incisors, they will not come into full wear until he is six years old. There is a long dark mark on the top of each tooth and this gradually fades and contracts until it disappears altogether at about the age of twelve, beginning with the two middle teeth and last seen on the "corner" incisors. At about eight years old the "fanghole" makes its first appearance as a long stain which in its turn contracts, but grows darker in colour, until about the age of twenty, after which no definite rule can be laid down. It is therefore possible to tell the exact age of a donkey until he is ten and estimate roughly thereafter until he is twenty. After that only the shape of the teeth gives any indication of his years. The shape changes all along with the age of the beast and this is really the easiest way for a beginner to find out whether the animal is old or young. Looked at from above, the teeth change from being long in a young mouth to almost completely triangular in a very old one. Looked at in profile, in a young animal the teeth of both jaws should meet evenly; even if they don't meet, the teeth are set more or less straight in the head. The older the donkey grows, the more his teeth begin to slope and the longer they get. You first really notice the 'slope' at about eight years old and thereafter some mouths seem to age more quickly than others. The teeth of a very old donkey may grow so long and pointed that they need to be rasped by a veterinary surgeon once or twice a year. Page 20 shows diagrams of the six teeth.

There is an old rhyme about telling the age of a horse which is catchy and fairly, if not very, helpful, and it seems worth reproducing it here:

To tell the age of any horse,
Inspect the lower jaw, of course;
The six front teeth the tale will tell,
And every doubt and fear dispel.

Two middle "nippers" you behold
Before the colt is two weeks old.
Before eight weeks two more will come;
Eight months the "corners" cut the gum.

The outside grooves will disappear
From middle two in just one year.
In two years from the second pair;
In three, the corners too are bare.

At two the middle "nippers" drop,
At three, the second pair can't stop.
When four years old the third pair goes;
At five a full new set he shows.

The deep black spots will pass from view
At six years from the middle two.
The second pair at seven years;
At eight the spot each "corner" clears.

From middle "nippers" upper jaw,
At nine the black spots will withdraw.
The second pair at ten are white,
Eleven finds the "corners" light.

As time goes on, the horsemen know
The oval teeth three-sided grow;
They longer get, project before,
Till twenty, when we know no more.

If you feel you can't master the art of judging by the teeth, then look at the donkey's general appearance and in particular at his feet. The younger the animal is, the smaller and neater should be his hooves. This isn't, unfortunately, infallible, as many donkeys suffer from neglected feet which can become quite misshapen even at the age of three or four years old.

However, don't worry about age too much unless you want a young Jenny to breed from. Donkeys live a long time — up to thirty years or more — so that getting an obviously old animal doesn't mean that he will pass away the following year; and although it's not always easy to get her in foal after the age of ten or eleven if she hasn't foaled before, you can breed from a Jenny up till the age of twenty, with the proviso, of course, that she is in good shape physically.

If the donkey is to be a pet and not primarily intended for riding, there is much to be said for getting a very young one of about six months or upwards, which is the age at which in general they first come on the market. The main factor to be remembered here is that it must not be ridden until it is two years old and even then not over much until it is at least two and a half. You can lift a light child onto the back of an eighteen month old donkey for a few moments but do not do more than this or its back will be injured. The advantages of buying such a youngster lie in the fact that you have his training to yourself. Lead him around on a halter at the age when he is most dependent on you and you'll reap the benefits when he is fully grown. Also, he may come from an unknown source and you will have his health in your own hands right from the start. Have his feet trimmed at regular intervals, give him a worming dose twice a year, keep his coat groomed, and you will never have to learn what a long time it can take to get a poor-conditioned animal back into health.

Now for the size of the donkey, which hasn't necessarily anything to do with his age. The average height of a donkey is about ten hands (four inches to a hand measured at the withers). However the breed ranges from the miniature for which the upper limit has been set at 36 inches to the large Spanish type which is over 12 hands. What size of donkey you want is for you to decide, as it depends on your own taste and on what you want him for.

You will find that he comes in several colours, too. Grey is, of course, the most usual colour in Britain, but there are variations even in this, the range being from silver to light blonde. Black or dark brown donkeys are not quite so common and it is also possible to find them piebald, skewbald, pure white (with a stripe or albino) or red chestnut. All of these last four are uncommon and you have to pay more for them accordingly. It seems true to say that all donkeys have the famous "Cross" on their withers — except perhaps albinos, which by definition lack all pigment. The length and clearness of this mark varies exceedingly; some animals bear it most distinctly, curving right down their shoulders almost to the top of the foreleg, and with a fine dark stripe running the length of their spine as well until it vanishes in the tail. Sometimes a donkey with a particularly well-defined mark will have stripey legs that make one think of a quagga. At the other extreme, the "Cross" is sometimes very difficult to make out; in a white donkey, for instance, it may only be possible to distinguish it very faintly when the coat is wet. In black donkeys, of course, the mark is invisible, but in very dark brown or nearly black donkeys, the "Cross" is plainly there in a darker shade.

When the time comes for the actual purchase of the donkey, here are a few points which should help the complete amateur to pick out one that seems healthy. But do let me add that should you venture to buy a poor-looking sad little beast, it is very rewarding to see it regain health and confidence in human nature. Get your vet to have a look at it, give it a dose of worm mixture and repeat after a fortnight, provide ample fodder, and persist in talking to it quietly and often, with a regular titbit. Most of the wretched animals one sees all too often at horse fairs, could be transformed after a month or two of this treatment.

The very best way to tell a healthy animal is by his general appearance: if he looks miserable, then something is wrong. (It may have been maltreatment or starvation but is more likely to be worms).

A dull coat, hanging head, a pot belly on an otherwise thin body, excessive thinness all over — all these signs can point to bad worm infestation. All the horse family carry some worms but the condition becomes dangerous if allowed to go too far.

Look out for coughing, which could mean lung worms or even bronchitis; on the other hand it could be nothing but a temporary chill or perhaps a bit of dry straw tickling its throat — again, look at the general appearance of the beast.

Look at the eyes and nostrils: should they be exuding mucus, it might mean a bad chill or possibly something worse such as strangles (see chapter on Ailments).

Take note of the feet. They should be neat and small but all too often they appear completely misshapen or very long. Lameness caused by this condition can usually be remedied by careful trimming by a blacksmith, but if too far gone, it is not possible to restore the hoof to its right shape.

Bare patches in the animal's coat nearly always mean lice. This condition is not too dreadful from the human point of view as the lice do not affect us. Treatment is effective and fairly quick so do not be too put off by what can be a very unsightly appearance.

Don't be dismayed by such a list of pitfalls. All but an exceptionally bad worm case are potentially curable. There are, of course, more uncommon ailments, but if you are a nervous purchaser, I should advise you to get some knowledgeable person to accompany you, or a veterinary surgeon to look at the animal, if this can be arranged.

Lastly, while on the business of choosing, there is the question of shape and looks. The picture entitled "the Forward Seat" which faces page 65 is a rather bad photograph of a really good donkey. This Jenny, aged six years, is ten hands. She is strong-looking without being coarse, and note the line of her back, which has just enough depression to make bare-back riding comfortable without being an armchair. She was picked out on looks at a horse-fair in Ireland and is now producing a line of good-lookers. The shape of the back is an important factor if the donkey is intended for bare-back riding by children. Some have a 'ridge' back, rather like a cow, which is disguised by a saddle but can be most uncomfortable without any protection for the seat.

So much for finding and choosing a donkey. There follows the important question of how to get it home. If you buy from a dealer, he will probably deliver it for you at a small extra charge; otherwise it is usually easy enough to arrange with any firm of livestock transporters, and if you can't find one of these for yourself, a firm of auctioneers would probably give you one or two names. Make sure that such a firm will undertake to deliver the animal to you the same day as they collect it and that it will not be left standing in a draughty horse-box overnight somewhere. Of course, if the donkey is a small one and you own a van or a landrover, you can fit up the back to accommodate him. Make sure there is plenty of padding and straw in case he is nervous and shifts about; but they are sensible animals and usually stay quiet when in a tight corner. Loading up can be tricky in this case and you will need a certain amount of assistance and initiative so as to make sure the donkey doesn't injure itself whilst being got in. The loading is greatly facilitated in a case like this by backing the van up to a bank and getting the passenger in from the same level rather than up a makeshift gang-plank.

Incidentally, there are one or two tricks to be learnt which are invaluable in getting an obstinate or frightened animal into an ordinary horse-box. Placing his feet on the ramp is the great thing here: once this has been achieved it is usually fairly easy to get him on up and into the box. Sometimes is is easiest to lift his feet for him and place them on the ramp yourself. (The ramp can by the way, be made to look less formidable to his eyes if it is covered by straw). Do not use too much force without making sure that his feet are firmly placed or he could slip and injure himself, or a foot can get trapped under the bottom of the ramp). If he fights and refuses to mount, you will find that one of four different methods is sure to work.

1) Get the assistance of two people with a rope. Each of them should hold an end standing behind and on different sides of the donkey so that the rope lies under his tail and against his

quarters. They should then walk forward while you pull on his halter from in front, so that the rope drags against his behind, a feeling which he dislikes very much and which generally makes him move forward. If you have only one assistant, one end of the rope can be tied to the box while the assistant pulls on the other end.

2) Back the donkey in. Provided the animal is one which is willing to back easily in the ordinary way, this is probably the easiest method of all.

3) If you are on your own and unable to get anyone to help you, try blind-folding the donkey.

4) Try turning him round and round until he is thoroughly giddy.

Once inside the box it is wisest not to tie the donkey up, nor to leave the end of his halter rope trailing. This is a precaution against possible traffic accident; obviously the animal is less likely to be injured if his head is free in the case of a bad collision. Have a good bedding of straw in the box — both to avoid slipping and consequent injury, and also for warmth.

A donkey foal is usually very little trouble to transport as he can be taken fairly easily in the back of a reasonable-sized 4-door car, but someone should share the back seat with him in order to steady and reassure him by stroking and talking to him. However, this does depend on temperament; and if he happens to be very nervous and excitable, it is best not to transport him in this way, as he could break a leg while struggling in a cramped and unnatural position, and, one hardly need add, prove to be rather a hazard as a passenger.

CHAPTER THREE

Where to keep him

To keep a donkey you need a certain amount of space. It can be a paddock or part of a large garden but it should not be less than half an acre in extent and could with advantage be a good deal more. He needs this much space both for natural exercise and for the variation in diet it affords. It is also important from the point of view of the quality of the pasture itself, as the smaller it is, the sooner will it become "horse-sick". This means in reality that as well as being bare in patches where he has eaten the sweet grass, and rank where he has fouled, it is infested with the eggs of the worms passed out in his droppings. These live for some time and can be picked up again (Chapter 8 refers).

If you haven't got this much space, then you will have to contrive something to help out for part of the year. Perhaps a friend will have somewhere suitable to keep the donkey for short periods while his home paddock grows or while you fertilize or lime it. Liming, if appropriate, also has a certain destructive effect on the worm eggs. After liming, do not return the donkey to his paddock until the rain has washed it into the ground a bit — it is not poisonous, but too much is not very good for the system.

Once the question of 'where' to keep the donkey is decided, there is the question of 'how' — in other words, what sort of fencing! Donkeys are, generally speaking, more 'escape conscious' than horses, and it's no good hoping that a few poles and a bit of rusty wire will show him which side of the fence is his. Unsupported hedging is not satisfactory either from your point of view, as the donkey will regard it as supplementary diet. This raises another very important point. If there is a hedge or tree incorporated in the paddock or within three or four feet of the fence, be sure that it is not yew, laurel, rhododendron or other injurious evergreen. Of these, yew is the most dangerous, as even a very small quantity can cause a most painful death within an hour or two. Dead yew is even more effectively poisonous than living. So if you have a yew or other danger-

ous tree or shrub, make sure that it is fenced right off — more than a neck's length away from temptation.

Unquestionably, the most satisfactory fencing is post and rails, but it is, of course, more expensive than wire. Three or four strands of plain wire, tightly stretched by someone who knows how to do it, make an efficient fence. So, of course, does barbed wire. There are disadvantages to barbed wire, however, as it can cause injuries, but there is no doubt that it is a relatively cheap and effective form of fencing, particularly if you are in a hurry or have a large area to enclose. Perhaps the best and most economical solution is to use two

C

strands of barbed wire with a top strand of plain wire.

Opinions seem to differ about the effectiveness of electric fencing with donkeys. We have never used it ourselves, but understand that whereas some people find it perfectly satisfactory, others regard it as useless. Perhaps it depends on how thick the donkey's skin is!

Whatever fencing you decide upon, and I do recommend some form of wooden fencing if you can afford it, remember that it is important to keep the lowest rail or strand of wire near to the ground — about 12 ins. away is usual, as donkeys are good crawlers. But do not be deceived into thinking that he hasn't the makings of a jumper : he probably has if circumstances seem to him worthwhile. A small donkey doesn't mean a low fence, and all fences should therefore be a good 3 ft. 6 ins. in height.

Lastly, while on this important question of fencing, remember to avoid having sharp stakes or iron railing posts as these can cause terrible wounds if the donkey does attempt to jump the barrier and fails to clear it.

By and large, it seems to follow that the smaller the area of your enclosure, the more the donkey will want to find new pasture, and consequently, the more effective the fencing will have to be. He is very intelligent and quite capable of working out ways of getting himself out of his paddock. I was told the other day of a donkey who had somehow learnt to cross over a cattle grid by keeping close to the sides.

Speaking in the short term, it is possible, of course, to tether the animal for a few hours at a time in a convenient spot, but it is not wise to go away from the premises if you do this, as he can tie himself into an elaborate cat's cradle of rope

in a quite short while. There are three important things to remember about tethering. First, he should be wearing either a leather headstall or a rope halter with a fixed knot (see Chapter 9 on Tack). If the noseband is on a slip knot, he can stifle himself if he pulls hard on the rope or steps on it. Secondly, make sure that the tethering rope is tied to something firm or you will find the donkey later in the kitchen garden or some other equally unsuitable spot. A donkey I was told of some years ago was much addicted to washing hanging out to dry, and on one occasion was found to have eaten the arms of six shirts.

Thirdly, stretch the tethering rope to its full extent yourself before tying the donkey up — this is to ensure that he is really out of reach of anything he can damage or anything that could damage him.

A donkey will share a field happily with horses, cattle or sheep — in fact he is supposed to have a steadying influence on other animals and is sometimes kept with thoroughbred horses for this reason. From the point of view of his own welfare, however, pasture-sharing with horses or cattle is preferable to sharing with sheep. This is because sheep's urine taints the pasture, thus rendering it rather unpalatable to other animals.

CHAPTER FOUR

Feeding

Summer

Herbage is a donkey's daily bread and one cannot stress sufficiently that he should have plenty of it available. With only a small paddock this is the great difficulty. You can, of course, supplement what there is with hay, but don't forget that this is a winter diet and in the summer you should try to work out some way of getting him fresh food. Quite apart from this, you will find that summer is your own easy season — you may be glad enough to be able to stop the daily routine of feeding hay.

Now, although I am speaking of grass as all-important, it doesn't mean that donkeys are fastidious. One of their great merits is their willingness to eat all kinds of rough herbage including brambles and briars. The last two named act as roughage and are in fact good for them. The bark of young trees and saplings is, unfortunately, also a taste that appeals, so if you are keeping a donkey in an orchard, take the precaution of covering the trunks of young trees with netting wire; he is not likely to touch the bark of older trees unless very hungry. Almost all kinds of meadow plants are liked except docks, excess of buttercups and ragwort. It is worthwhile getting rid of the latter, as it is bad for stock, although they rarely touch it. Rather than use a weed-killer, try pulling it up by the roots. It is quite easy to do this, and a few minutes a day spent on this task will clear any field effectively in the end (as we have proved). Be sure to gather up the stalks as you go, as dead ragwort is more dangerous than the growing plant. Nettles are among the weeds that are much liked, but although some donkeys seem to relish them as they grow, others won't eat them until they have been cut down and left to dry for the day.

Rich grass and a great deal of clover does not suit donkeys, so don't be deterred because you think your paddock has poor quality grass, and feel that you must re-sow it; it will probably be quite suitable for a donkey. Lush, long grass is usually left if they have the alternative of short grass. Over-rich grass and clover often lead to skin troubles such as eczema.

It is up to you to judge how much fodder there is growing in your paddock and whether the occupant is going hungry. In a small enclosure, a little contrivance at the beginning of the growing season can save worry later on. As soon as the grass begins to grow strongly — usually during the first half of April (but this depends on the season) — see if you can get your animal quartered elsewhere for two or three weeks and let the growth really get going. Incidentally, once you have located an alternative pasture, remember to check it for possible dangers such as yew, or bits of rusty barbed wire left lying about; also ensure that there is a water supply. Don't let his home grass grow too long and lush because if he is suddenly introduced back into it from poor pasture, he may get laminitis (see Chapter 8).

If you have got a paddock of reasonable proportions, one way to help with the problem of letting the grass grow a bit is to divide the area and let the donkey live in one half at a time. Imagination used over this kind of thing will make all the difference to his health and fitness.

Water

It is most important not to neglect the question of a water supply. It should be always available as some donkeys prove to be thirsty characters. They are rather fastidious about water too, so don't think that some rusty old bath that has never been cleaned out will be adequate. Scrub out the container frequently unless it is a proper trough, and even then every month or so. Standing water should be renewed every day. Spring water or rain water is always preferred to hard tap water and is in fact better for animals, but of course it isn't always possible to supply this. Never have the drinking tank made of lead, as animals can get lead-poisoning from the water which becomes contaminated.

Salt

All ponies and donkeys benefit from having a salt lick, and it is a want that is very easily satisfied. Buy a lump of rock salt from your local agricultural merchants (some sell it in special holders which you can nail on to a fence or the wall of the stall). If it is just in lump form, put it in a dry corner under cover. It will last for a long time and is just the sort of extra attention which tells on condition.

Winter

However much land you have allocated to your donkey, in winter you will need to supplement his diet. There is little goodness in grass at this time of the year and it has to be remembered that it doesn't grow at all while the temperature is below 40°F; in other words, there is virtually no growth during December, January and February and very little in late November and early March, although of course this does depend on the mildness of the season. For the best part of five months, therefore, the donkey will depend on hay as his main food.

If you have somewhere to store it, it is a good idea to buy your hay in bulk in the late summer or early autumn, as prices gradually rise during the colder months. Provided he has not less than an acre of pasture to nibble about in, a large bale of hay should last one donkey for about six days during the three coldest months. The smaller the area he lives in, the more hay he will need. You will soon know if you are giving him too much, as he will feed messily, leaving bits lying about. Begin feeding him a little hay during the first half of November and gradually build up the quantity, decreasing it again towards the end of March. Unless it is a very late spring, you can usually stop feeding hay by mid-April. During snow he will, of course, need more hay than his usual ration.

Baled hay is a blessing to those trying to estimate quantities, although unfortunately the size of different contractors' bales varies considerably. Loose hay is harder to store as well as to apportion. Calculating in large bales, the following is a rough estimate of the needs of one donkey kept on an acre of land, over the five winter months:

Eating at the rate of one bale to six days over a period of 150 days, a donkey will require twenty-five bales. As half a ton will contain at least twenty-five bales, this is a convenient quantity to order and should be an adequate winter's supply.

If you live in the country it is usually easy enough to buy hay from a farmer in the neighbourhood, and in more built-up areas it is not so difficult as you might suppose. The advertising column of your local paper is often helpful, or you can always ask any large firm of agricultural merchants to arrange for you to be supplied. It pays to get good quality first-year meadow hay. Beware of old hay; sometimes friends will offer you hay which has grown musty in their barn for years and this can be quite dangerous as fodder. If practicable, it is a good plan to look at hay before you buy it unless you are very sure about its origin. Good hay should smell sweet and it is quite easy to detect mouldy and old hay both by its dark and dusty colour as well as by a musty odour. If the bales are inclined to make you want to sneeze, that is a sure sign that it is too old for feeding.

If you are going to store the winter's hay supply yourself, make sure that it is in a weatherproofed shed, or else that it is securely covered by a tarpaulin; with small quantities you can't afford to waste any. A tarpaulin makes great sport for the winds, so rope it down well. If the stack is to be out of doors, build it on hard-standing if at all possible or you will lose the bottom bales through damp. It is advisable, too, to make the stack well out of reach of the donkey himself or you will find him taking extra rations.

As regards the routine of feeding, the short winter days and long nights must be monotonous for field animals. Feeding time is always a high spot so try to arrange two hand-outs of hay during the day, morning and evening. Apart from anything else, this is better for the animal, as it spreads the ration out to correspond more naturally to the normal intervals of feeding all round the clock. Put the hay either in a manger, in a hay net hung at head level, or on the ground, provided, in the latter instance, that you don't dump it down in the muddiest corner of the field or on a place covered with droppings. If you are using baled hay, shake it out well, as it comes out of the bale in tight wedges.

It may not be necessary to give further food supplements to donkeys except during prolonged wet weather or snow, but there is no doubt that they are beneficial to his general condition and, of course, they are greatly liked.

The easiest supplement of all to feed is 'Horse and Pony Cubes'. These contain proteins and minerals otherwise absent from winter feeding. Feed them throughout the three coldest months at the rate of a cupped handful every day: do *not* give more than this, however, as an excess of protein is harmful.

Our donkeys' favourite stand-by in the way of a food supplement is bran mash. During really inclement weather, you will find that it is very popular indeed and is a good precaution against chills. Mix four cupped handfuls of broad bran and one of crushed oats with enough boiling or very hot water to form a moist but not too wet consistency, and let the mixture steam under a cloth for five minutes or so. A little glucose added (say a tablespoonful) is a good stimulant to a donkey that is off colour. Don't feed more oats than the quantity mentioned, as they are rather rich for donkeys. Remember that in any case they must be *crushed* oats, as whole oats are extremely indigestible.

Flaked maize makes a good addition to a bran mash instead of oats, but again, don't overdo it — a cupped handful to a mash is quite sufficient.

Another good winter feed which has plenty of body is beet pulp, but it must be prepared with care or the results will be disastrous. Be sure that it is soaked in water for at least half a day before feeding it, as it swells enormously and unless fully swollen beforehand will continue to swell inside the donkey's stomach. Feed it at the rate of a cupped handful a day. This is part of the waste product of sugar beet and isn't easy to get hold of in all districts.

During the winter, titbits of apples and carrots, and extras such as the outer leaves of cabbages and cauliflowers, are particularly welcome to an animal when he lacks the freshness of grass. Swedes or turnips are often liked as a novelty, and if they go down well, can be given regularly.

Water

There is another important point to remember about winter care: don't forget that a donkey can't break the ice on his water trough himself. He needs more water when he is living mainly on dry hay, so check his water supply morning and evening during frosts.

Titbits

This seems a good moment to introduce the subject of titbits. Donkeys, like any other animal, tend to have individual tastes, and you will soon find out your own pet's preferences. Generally speaking, apples, carrots and vegetable peelings are the things most liked and the things best for him. On the whole, beware of kitchen scraps except for those mentioned, as he may be greedy enough to eat things which are quite unsuitable or dangerous, such as something containing meat. Bread and buns are safe, but fattening in large quantities, so try to restrict him to the hard crusty bits. Another unnatural food which should not be overdone is lump sugar — Glucose is better for him.

The secret of our own especial titbit, our "recette de maison" so to speak, was revealed to us by the former owners of our first donkeys. It has proved so popular with all other donkeys I have met, that it seems worthwhile passing it on. The magic word is "peppermint". I think it can be safely stated that the way to any donkey's heart lies through a tube or bag of any of the well-known brands of white peppermints.

CHAPTER FIVE

Shelter and bedding

A DONKEY is not quite such a hardy animal as his appearance suggests. He is not a native of these islands, and although he flourishes in Ireland it must be remembered that the climate of that country is considerably milder than that of the rest of the British Isles. This should be borne in mind when someone tells you that their pony lives out without shelter all the year round. The particular pony probably belongs to one of our native breeds and is better adapted to the cold and damp of our winters than the donkey, although I would add that some sort of shelter seems to be desirable for any animal. In natural conditions, it would, after all, seek the cover of trees or rocks during wild weather, but it is all too often kept in some open field without any kind of protection from wind and rain.

For a donkey, a shelter of some kind is really essential in the winter and is very desirable also in the summer as the best means of preventing flies tormenting him during hot days. For some reason these pests do leave animals alone while in the semi-darkness of a stall or shed. I am not suggesting that you shut the donkey in during the day, but simply that a house should be available. Our donkeys of their own choice spend the major part of

every hot day half asleep in their shelter during July and August.

There need be nothing particularly difficult or costly about getting a shelter. It is surprising how often you find that there is something on the premises which will do or which can be converted; you may have an unwanted shed which can be taken down and re-erected without too much outlay. Donkeys are not very large, and therefore the house need not be very high, although when it comes to cleaning it out, it will be much more labour-saving if it is high enough for you to move about in comfortably. A chicken house can be converted without a great deal of difficulty by someone who is handy, simply by raising the roof: don't worry if there is a step up into it, as donkeys can negotiate this perfectly easily. Best of all you may have an outhouse actually alongside part of the paddock and can extend the fence to include it, or have a new door made if the old one is on the wrong side.

Any simple shelter will be better than nothing, provided it doesn't face directly into the prevailing wind and isn't full of holes and gaps. (Draughts can do more damage than an open wind to livestock). Ideally it should be four-sided with a doorway (and a half-door) so that the donkey can get right away from the wind and rain. The roof, covered with roofing felt or a similar water-proofed material, should be sloped (but not from back to front) so that the rain can run off. It pays to give all the timber-work of the shed a thorough painting with Stockholm tar or creosote. This has the double effect of preserving it against damp rot and also of deterring woodworm and other wood-boring insects. Both these treatments smell strongly, and it is advisable to do your painting well in advance of the shed's occupation, or the tenant may be somewhat put off.

Directions for building a simple type of shelter from scratch are given at the end of this chapter. Choose the site with care, with natural shelter if possible, and fix on a well-drained spot. The foundation should be hard; an earth floor is not practicable as it becomes impossible to clean out properly. If it is on a new site, have a concrete floor laid down or at least have it made of good stout planking. The latter cannot be regarded as a permanent flooring as old planking is dangerous when it begins to rot and the animal may put his foot through the floor and injure himself. If you are using concrete, be generous and give a small concrete standing outside the door, as this place tends to become very soggy in winter with constant passage to and fro. It will also pay to make a concrete base for your hay supply if it is standing out of doors.

As regards the use of the shelter, let the donkey regulate his own habits. He is quite capable of deciding for himself when it is best to stay in and when to come out, unless, of course, he is ill. Don't start keeping him in at night in the winter and then let him out a few evenings later because you think it is milder; this is asking for trouble, and in any case he is a better judge of temperature than you are. Cold winter rain is the thing he hates most, but sharp frosts rarely bother him. Donkeys vary considerably in their habits, and while some use their houses a great deal, others seem to be more hardy. If for some reason you want to keep your donkey in at night in winter, go through with the job and go on keeping him in every night until spring has really arrived; but I must emphasize that this is rarely necessary with a donkey unless he is a very weakly animal. If it is, a half door is essential. Never shut him in completely without fresh air, even for short periods.

Straw makes the best bedding and is the most usual. It can be bought in the same way as hay, ready baled, and in country areas many farmers are glad to sell it to you straight from the field in this condition. A bale of straw goes quite a long way, and in a small stall about twenty bales should last comfortably through the winter, when for warmth the bedding needs to be thicker than in summer. Only wheat or oat straw should be used, and never barley. Animals tend to nibble at bedding, and barley straw is dangerous because of its brittle and prickly nature. Incidentally, you will find the strawy manure much in demand for your neighbours' gardens once you have liberally supplied your own.

Dried bracken can be used as bedding, but

D

only if the donkey has plenty of hay available, as he may eat the bracken, and too much can be bad for him. Sawdust and wood-shavings both make good bedding if used in sufficient quantity, but are not usually very easy to get hold of.

Clean out the bedding regularly. Apart from the fact that it is bad for hooves to stand in damp muck every time he goes indoors, you will find that it is much easier this way than waiting till the straw is sodden and filthy. Have the manure heap near the shelter to save trouble but do not have it actually standing outside the door, as it will attract flies.

A last word about the use of a shelter: if you intend to go in for breeding donkeys, it is a good idea to have it fitted with an infra-red heater, high up on the wall or in the ceiling. Its use, one would hope, would be rare, but if a foal is ill it can be difficult to keep it sufficiently warm without artificial heat. We have tried wrapping a four month old filly in an eiderdown — an experiment which seemed to keep the animal warm enough but which had disastrous effects on the eiderdown. By the way, if you do pin a wrapping over a donkey foal, fasten it with "nappy" safety pins.

How to build a simple shed:

The minimum floor area to allow the donkey to turn comfortably and give him fresh air is about 7 ft. by 7 ft. with a doorway 2 ft. 6 ins. wide. For your own convenience when working inside the shed it must be at least 6 ft. high at the highest point. The simplest possible shed will look something like this:-

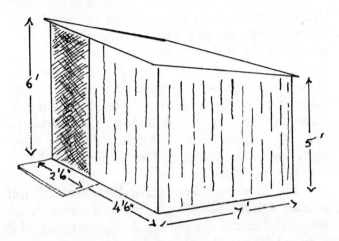

Taking the above dimensions, you will need for the floor:

At least 3 "yards" (cubic yards) of wall ballast

At least 10 cubic feet of ready-mixed concrete

And for the shed:

3   8 ft. front uprights (4 ins. by 4 ins.)

2   7 ft. back uprights (4 ins. by 4 ins.)

5   7 ft. 6 ins. cross braces (3 ins. by 2 ins.)

3   7 ft. 6 ins. battens (2 ins. by 1 in.)

1   4 ft. 6 ins. batten

About 50 6 ft. offcuts (the pieces of timber nearest to the bark which are left over when cutting planks)

3 pieces of corrugated iron 7 ft. 6 ins. long for roof

A quantity of roofing felt.

First of all sharpen the uprights if necessary and soak the bottom 2 ft. 6 ins. in creosote for 24 hours. Mark out an area 8 ft. square with an extension of about 3 ft. square opposite the intended doorway and dig out the top 6 ins. of top soil. Drive in the corner up-rights so that their outer edges are 7 ft. apart and they stand 5 ft. and 6 ft. respectively above natural soil level; the third front upright can then be sited and driven in 2 ft. 6 ins. from one of the others to form a doorway. Make sure they are vertical.

Fill in the cavity with wall-ballast and roll or ram it level, ramming particularly firmly near the uprights. Do not put on the concrete yet as it may crack with the movement of the posts as you hammer other parts onto them.

Next tie the tops of the posts with your 3 ins. by 2 ins. cross braces, doing front and back first and laying the side braces, and one in the centre, on top of them. This will leave a small air gap at the top which is beneficial. Then nail your battens horizontally about half way up the posts, using the short one, of course, for the front. Trim all overlaps. Then sort out your offcuts so that they fit each side and each other as neatly as possible. Trim the side ones to allow for the slope of the roof — this need not be too exact as you will be leaving a space anyway — and site the nails, hammering them just through the offcuts on the ground in order to save strain on the framework. Then fix them to the frame.

Finally attach your roof of corrugated iron sheets, overlapping them neatly and closely; leave a projection of 3 ins. all round to form eaves. Cover any chinks between the offcuts inside the shed with roofing felt, tacking it well down, since the donkey may amuse himself by tearing at loose corners.

You are then ready to cover the floor with concrete, level it, fill up cavities under the offcuts and leave it to set. The concrete must be strong enough to bear the considerable weight which a donkey puts on its small hoof. On a wall-ballast foundation an average depth of 1 in. should be enough, but if you were laying it direct on to the soil, you would need at least 2 ins., and this could mean that the saving of labour had involved you in considerable extra expense.

The whole job is neither so laborious nor so expensive as it may sound, but if you wish you can economise in both money and labour. Instead of the rather expensive 4 ins. by 4 ins. posts, you can use stout chestnut poles about 6 ins. in diameter treated with creosote in the same way; but to make a reasonably neat and draught-proof job of it you will have to cut notches to take the battens. Again, you can leave out the battens and offcuts altogether and use straw bales for the sides, but this must be regarded as a temporary measure and you will have to replace them quite frequently. Finally, you can use stout sound planking for the flooring, provided you raise it off the soil with bricks or wooden transverse poles and inspect it periodically to ensure that it is not becoming dangerous.

CHAPTER SIX

Care of hooves and coat

The hoof

Donkeys should have the neatest possible little hooves, but unfortunately one sees them in this condition only too rarely. Their original habitat in Asia is hard and stony ground and it is probably for this reason that a donkey's feet get misshapen more quickly than those of ponies when living in our lush English meadows. Until recently, of course, the domesticated donkey has been used as a working animal, and road work in itself keeps unshod hooves roughly pared to a certain extent.

It certainly is unnecessary to have a donkey shod unless you propose to use him for a lot of road work. To keep his hooves correctly shaped, however, you must have them pared regularly. Once they have gone too far, it will be impossible to get them looking perfect again. Correct shape is of course, primarily a matter of comfort — the donkey's whole gait is affected by the condition of his feet. Misshapen hooves give a most unsightly appearance, but the worst thing about them is that they cause him to walk on the wrong part of his foot and consequently to go lame. The mass of hoof accumulating in front will prevent him from walking on the sole and push him back on to his heel or on to the inner side of the hoof, so that his whole body is wrongly balanced on his legs. I have seen a Jenny donkey, now in happy circumstances, who was discovered lying down, scarcely able to rise, owing to goodness knows how many years of neglect to her feet. The animal, which was past hobbling, was bought by an acquaintance who, after considerable attention, managed to restore to it the use of its legs. It seems that it will never be able to walk about freely but only with a kind of cramped shuffle.

One of the illustrations on page 56 depicts a hoof that has been left to grow too long. Almost as bad as this, or worse, is the hoof which has been sawn off with something out of the home tool chest and has been cut back far too much, damaging the quick. Again, the foot which has been cut in such a way may never regain its proper shape, or at any rate not for a year or two, and may develop a vertical crack. In addition, as the sawing off must have been painful, the donkey is most likely to be permanently shy of a blacksmith or anyone else who handles its hooves.

Vertical cracks, which are due to faulty rasping by a blacksmith or some untrained person, or to an injury, can only be remedied by a black-

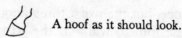

A hoof as it should look.

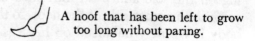

A hoof that has been left to grow too long without paring.

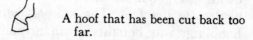

A hoof that has been cut back too far.

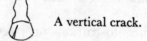

A vertical crack.

A hoof with a dropped sole — a sign that the donkey suffers from laminitis.

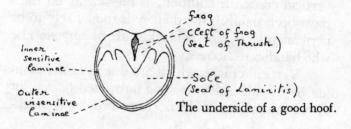

The underside of a good hoof.

smith. He will stop the crack developing by making a groove across the top of the crack, and in time it will usually grow out.

The next illustration shows a hoof with a dropped sole. This probably means that the donkey has suffered from laminitis (see Chapter 8), and the hoof generally remains slightly deformed, although the donkey's gait will not be affected.

The way to avoid all these troubles, except the last named, is to have the donkey's feet pared regularly by a blacksmith (also known as a farrier), four times a year being the absolute minimum; it should be done every two months. Frequency does, however, depend a bit both on the animal and on your land. A mare heavy in foal, kept in a low-lying and rather soggy meadow, will need attention twice as often as a young animal kept on firm grassland. A blacksmith doesn't charge much for paring hooves but the chief difficulty is usually to find one to do it, as from his point of view it is a very small job. Blacksmiths are rather few and far between nowadays, and they nearly all come to the horses instead of vice-versa. The best way to make contact with one of them is to get in touch with someone in your neighbourhood who keeps ponies and to ask their farrier to come to you at the same time that he visits them. He will usually oblige you willingly enough if you can arrange it this way. Should you find yourself unable to locate a blacksmith in your area, your vet will probably be able to recommend one to you.

Generally speaking, a donkey foal will not need any attention to his hooves until he is about a year old, but it is sensible to let a smith handle his feet when he is attending to the mother, as this will get him used to it from the very beginning. Don't worry if a foal's feet seem to develop a horizontal groove across them, slowly growing lower down the foot — this is simply the hardening of the foot while the baby hoof grows out.

Do not, on any account, attempt to pare hooves yourself without prior instruction from a blacksmith or, which is just as important, without the right tools. It is easy to pare them the wrong way, and a task that looks so skilfully and quickly done by an expert, can prove crippling when handled by an amateur.

Donkeys should have no fear of the smith and should give their feet easily and calmly to be trimmed. If, however, ill treatment has frightened the donkey before he came into your possession, get him accustomed to you feeling his legs and feet and picking up his hooves while talking to him. Gently scrape the soles of his feet with a piece of wood or something similar — in fact do anything to show him that foot handling doesn't mean pain. Don't, incidentally, try standing immediately behind a donkey, particularly a strange one, and pick up its back hoof to see if it minds. Always examine one of the front feet first and lift all feet from the side.

The inside of a donkey's foot is very vulnerable to thorns and nails, and a hoof-pick, which can be bought very cheaply, is an invaluable asset. It picks out mud from the hoof far more effectively than any other instrument and enables you to discover whether the animal is lame from a wound in the frog of the foot, a pebble picked up and embedded, or from some other cause (see Chapter 8 for diseases affecting the foot).

The Coat

Not many people bother to groom a donkey regularly but with his thick hair a good hard brushing once a week does bear results both in appearance and in the discouragement to lice.

Donkeys are, in fact, rather coat-conscious and if you keep two of them together, you will notice that they spend a good deal of time grooming each other with their teeth. Their other way of keeping their coats in order is by rolling. They love to do this and if you want to provide a permanent source of pleasure, give them a heap of sand to roll in. They will always choose sand for preference if given the chance, but without it will usually select a certain spot for rolling where gradually the grass wears away and a kind of dust bowl is formed. This becomes mud in the winter but they continue to roll and emerge blanketed with it.

Donkeys tend to be either the shaggy or non-shaggy type. All of them grow winter coats, and usually the long rough hair begins to be cast in spring, and by summer they are comparatively short-haired and trim without any assistance, although grooming speeds it up. A few, on the other hand, seem to cling to their thick woolly coats however hot the summer. This is sometimes, but not necessarily, a matter of condition; casting the coat early usually being a sign of fitness. This raises the question of whether to have a shaggy donkey clipped or not. There is certainly something to be said for it from the point of view of keeping him clean and also if you are curious to see his real shape! However, be careful not to do it too early in the season unless he lives in; wait until June at least, or you may give him pneumonia or at any rate a severe chill. It doesn't appear to inconvenience him to remain long-haired throughout the summer, so don't worry about this point too much; you will discover by brushing his hair backwards along the spine, how clean his coat is. Some owners like their donkeys to look like small yaks but if they remain shaggy and ungroomed, an examination under the top hair will often show literally hundreds of louse eggs.

The best article for grooming a donkey is a dandy brush, and a rubber curry comb helps to get mud and tangles out; either can be bought at a saddler's. A 'body brush' is too soft for most donkey's coats, sliding over it rather than going through it. Keep a steel comb handy to clean out the brush, and when you have finished tap out the brush and comb on the floor; occasionally dip them in a disinfectant solution.

As well as keeping the coat clean and adding to the donkey's smart appearance, grooming is

good because it stimulates the blood vessels just below the skin, and these in turn produce glossier individual hairs. Once you have seen your donkey looking spruce and trim, you will probably feel a good deal more pride in him than in the dull-coated, slightly scruffy-looking animal he was before. Grooming also has the advantage of revealing little scabs and rough places where, perhaps, a thorn has penetrated the skin and is sticking. It can usually be eased out, but be careful not to leave in the point.

Use a curry comb or the steel comb to care for his mane and tail.

There are two parts of his body which are most important to a donkey and which are rarely attended to by his masters; these are the insides of his ears. There is a certain amount of hair inside the edges, and it collects various burrs and foreign objects which must be highly irritating to the animal who is unable to do much about it. If you want to transport a donkey to the pitch of ecstacy, rub the insides of his ears with your finger or with a bit of rag. He will stretch his head out and hold his neck quite rigid while you are doing it and you can practically feel him purring.

CHAPTER SEVEN

Pitfalls

NOT all dangers to the horse family are obvious ones. This short chapter attempts to mention those more common pitfalls which can be overlooked. I list them alphabetically — not in order of importance; in fact, as far as poisons are concerned, the last-mentioned, i.e. yew, should rank first.

Acorns. These are bad if eaten in quantity. Don't worry about the odd small oak tree overhanging the paddock, which sheds a few acorns; but if you find that there really is a great number of acorns lying about, take the trouble to sweep them up.

Bracken. This appears to be a slightly mysterious plant in that it is eaten in quantity by some donkeys without affecting them in any visible way whatever, whereas it can cause a swift drop in condition in others. In fact, it is highly alkaline and only becomes dangerous if the alkaline content in some animals' systems becomes built up above the safety level. Incidentally, donkeys seem to relish it most when it is fully grown and dark green and rank-looking, rather than when it is young and tender.

Evergreens. Beware of all evergreens: many of them are poisonous and most of them indigestible. (Rhododendrons and cherry laurel are two of the worst).

Garden waste. It is better to avoid feeding any garden clippings and waste, as various cultivated plants and roots (such as irises) are poisonous and, being unfamiliar, may tempt a donkey to sample them.

Hay. As already mentioned, in Chapter 4, mouldy and very old hay is bad and may lead to colic (Chapter 8).

Holes. Rabbit holes and diggings, etc., are most dangerous if the field is used for riding the donkey, as he can easily put his foot in one of them and break a leg. Left to himself, he usually has the sense to avoid such traps, but they are still best filled in.

Laburnum. These trees may grow beside or in your donkey's paddock. Their seeds and leaves are very poisonous, so fence them off securely.

Lawn mowings. A danger, very frequently not recognised, is a heap of fresh lawn mowings given to eat. These generate great heat if piled up: you have only to put your hand into them on the compost heap to realise this. They will similarly generate heat inside an animal's stomach. If you really want to feed them to your donkey for one reason or another, let it be a small quantity at a time and scatter them about on the ground.

Lead poisoning. This can be acquired through drinking water which has stood in a lead-lined trough. Drinking troughs should never contain lead.

Ragwort. Already mentioned in Chapter 4. It is not readily eaten by stock, but as it is a common weed and causes slow poisoning if they do start eating it, it should be eliminated from the paddock. (It is more poisonous dead than growing, so don't leave it lying about).

Stake wounds. Caused by pointed railings or stakes in a fence if the donkey jumps out (see Chapter 3). They can be very nasty indeed and even fatal.

String. Always take off the string from baled hay before pulling it apart or you may forget and later find it partly swallowed along with a mouthful of hay. Also it is a menace left lying about, as a donkey can sprain his foot by getting tangled up in it.

'You must wrap up in this weather'

'I never could make her out!'

The forward seat

Rather more orthodox

Titbits. These can be a great source of worry, as well-intentioned people who pass your donkey's paddock often produce titbits without asking permission. They can be a real danger; for instance, they might contain meat; or they may be something extremely indigestible, such as sweets or chocolates still wrapped in silver paper.

Weeds. Many weeds are poisonous, but apart from those named in this chapter not under this heading, they are either not readily eaten or not very widespread. It would be impracticable to list them all here, but the following are common enough to record: hemlock, all nightshades, St. John's wort, spindle berries and spurge. It is probably safe to say that donkeys would not normally eat these plants unless they were very short of food.

Wire. Wire left lying about is a menace to anything, especially if it is barbed wire or rusty. Always check round a paddock for this if you are leasing one.

Yew. Among poisons, the chief plant of which to beware is yew — either green or its dead clippings, which are even more dangerous. Animals don't seem to know the danger of this tree, and it doesn't give them many chances — a very little can kill in a very short time. So if you have a yew tree or hedge within neck's reach of your donkey's paddock, put up an effective barrier.

E

CHAPTER EIGHT

Ailments

IN general donkeys are subject to much the same ailments as horses and ponies, and I cannot pretend to have listed them all. This chapter is devoted to recording the more usual complaints, and also difficulties connected with illness, which are likely to come within the average donkey-keeper's experience. It is important to remember that when in doubt you should call in the vet — even quite a small symptom may mean something serious: for example, listlessness could be a sign of heavy worm infestation; or bad breath an indication either of a rotten tooth (and toothache) or of kidney trouble. Generally speaking, a well-kept donkey is unlikely to become ill, so there is no need to go to the opposite extreme of taking his temperature every day! If it is necessary for you to take his temperature (which should incidentally read 100.4F), the thermometer should be placed in the rectum. The thermometer should preferably be a veterinary one and it is advisable to leave the task to the vet if possible as there is a danger of the instrument breaking if you are clumsy or the donkey makes a sudden movement.

A donkey in good condition should keep his ears pricked most of the time and they should feel warm to the touch. Flopping ears are not necessarily a sign of misery, but they often are; certainly they should not feel cold.

To give a horse medicine in liquid form is known as drenching. This should only be done by an amateur in an emergency: it is not easy and you will need help, the danger being that as a donkey's throat is narrow, the mixture may get into his lungs if he struggles violently. However, there may be an occasion when you have to do it. First get a bottle with a long thin neck and pour the dose into it. You will need the assistance of someone else (with a certain amount of strength) to hold the donkey's head up. Then slip the neck of the bottle well into the side of the mouth where there are no teeth; at the same place insert the thumb of your other hand and press the roof of the mouth. Give a little at a time, and leave a reasonable interval in between each gulp. If he refuses to swallow, you can induce this by smoothing his throat with one hand or by touching his tongue with your finger. If he starts to choke, remove the bottle and let his head down immediately.

In the case of a young foal, it may be willing to suck the drench from a baby's bottle, but if it tastes bad or the foal refuses, we find a good implement to use is a small rubber syringe. Push the nozzle into the corner of the mouth and squeeze in a little at a time, making sure that the foal swallows in between each squeeze and isn't holding it in its mouth. He should be standing unless he is too weak.

Occasionally a donkey is given a general anaesthetic by the veterinary surgeon, and it may be of assistance to know what to expect. The amount of anaesthetic given will depend on the assessment of the animal's body weight, but this is the concern of the vet. The donkey may be 'out' for some time, and as he will probably throw himself about when he is beginning to come round, you should stay near him all the time until he is fully conscious. A general anaesthetic should be given under cover if possible, and the animal should be lying on straw. Put some straw bales round him so that he doesn't injure himself when he begins to struggle to his feet. When coming round, he will at first open his eyes and lie quietly, obviously wondering what has hit him. Talk to him to re-assure him and when he begins to struggle to get up, take hold of his halter, then when he is actually on his feet, stand close to his head. He will be very staggery indeed at first and will probably want to lean against you! Walk about with him for a little while and then unhalter him and leave him on his own for an hour or two away from other animals until he has quite re-established his equilibrium.

Last rites. Should you be unlucky enough to lose a donkey through any doubtful cause, i.e. not from extreme old age, accident or an illness that has been treated by the vet, ask your vet to arrange an autopsy. It is better to know the cause of death and it may help others to avoid some pitfall.

If you have to have an animal destroyed, have it done on your own premises. Ponies and donkeys can stand about in knackers' yards for days, and there is no knowing where they will end up.

The following ailments are listed alphabetically and not in order of importance or commonness. At the end of the chapter there are some suggestions for equipping a simple 'medicine chest' and a list of some basic items which it is always useful to keep on hand.

Bots. These worm-like grubs are the larvae of the flies of the genus Galtrophilus. The eggs are laid on the donkey's hair — usually on his legs, but some species lay their eggs around the mouth and cheeks and on the lower jaw. The eggs laid on the host need to be licked or rubbed before they will hatch. They are thus transferred by the tongue to the mouth and then to the stomach. Here they grow and develop and the mature larvae are passed out through the back passage mainly in the spring, having spent ten or twelve months in the donkey's stomach. Once on the ground the larvae pupate and the adult flies emerge in three to five weeks during the later part of the summer. The larvae cause much irritation when they emerge, and the symptom is that of rubbing the backside frequently against a fence post or similar object.

The eggs can be found in the late summer on the legs, etc., and the adult larvae can be seen at the rectum in the spring, otherwise diagnosis is impossible. If you do spot these, consult your vet as to treatment.

Bronchitis. A complication resulting from a chill or influenza. Symptoms are coughing, shivering and quick and stifled breathing. Consult your vet and in the meantime keep the donkey warm inside his shed, without excluding fresh air.

Canker of the ear. Easily discovered as the donkey will hate to have the ear touched, and a flaky wax deposit can usually be seen inside. The vet will give you a preparation with which to dust the inside of the ear.

Chills and colds. These usually pass off naturally, but if the donkey's breathing is stifled and he is running at the nose and eyes, it will relieve him to hold his head with a towel over it above a pail of Friar's Balsam. A good hot mash last thing at night is also a good precaution against the chill developing into something worse such as pneumonia. If you bring him into his shed, be careful as usual not to shut him right in, thus depriving him of fresh air. Feed him his hay on the ground to give the mucus a chance to drain out of his nostrils. Donkeys sometimes shiver in heavy rain;

this doesn't necessarily mean that they are on the way to a bad chill, but keep an eye on them.

If a newly-arrived donkey is very runny at the nose, suspect strangles (dealt with later).

Colic. This has various causes, but those most likely to affect a donkey are a surfeit of very rich or new-mown grass, poisonous plants, unsuitable food, very heavy worm infestation, mouldy hay, or lack of access to water. The attack, which is sometimes very painful, should never last more than an hour or two. Symptoms are evident distress, prolonged and frequent rolling and kicking on the ground, and, while standing, trying to kick at his belly with his hind feet; also, looking round at his belly. The attack may pass quickly and of its own accord, but if it goes on after two hours, you should ring for the vet at once — particularly as complications, such as peritonitis, might set in. Should you be unable to get him, there is a simple home remedy which certainly gives some relief, but the administration has to be handled with great care (see Drenching). Mix half a pint of warm beer with a tablespoonful of whisky, and drench. Then walk him about gently and keep him quiet for a day or two.

Constipation. No sign of droppings for more than 24 hours may indicate something serious such as an impacted colon. Olive oil given as a drench may help but you should ask your vet to visit.

Eczema. This is non-contagious and can be caused by over-rich food, either in the form of 'feeds' containing, for instance, too many oats; or by over-luxuriant pasture with a high proportion of clover. The symptoms are extreme itchiness causing the donkey constantly to bite and rub itself. Scabs will develop on places that have been rubbed raw. First check the coat to see that it is free from lice — if this is the case, he is most probably suffering from eczema. Wash the affected parts with a mild disinfectant and feed bran mashes with a tablespoonful of Glauber salts mixed well in. If the animal obviously experiences no relief, consult your vet.

Enteritis. A dangerous illness, to which foals are particularly prone. It is usually caused by a chill on the stomach following cold rain, or by some unsuitable food. The signs are listlessness, burning or icy ears, and scouring. Get the donkey into a stall at once, keep him as warm as you can and send for the vet immediately. It is very hard to save a foal that has enteritis, and it is most distressing to nurse as he is often in a good deal of pain. He will need to be dosed at regular intervals with whatever is prescribed.

The Eyes. Any condition that causes watering of the eye or a thicker discharge for more than forty-eight hours, should always be treated with the utmost suspicion and advice sought. Take action sooner if the animal appears to be in pain or discomfort.

For treatment of eye sores caused by flies, see under the heading *Sores*.

Influenza. Symptoms are severe shivering and streaming of the nose as with a bad chill. Get the animal into its shed and treat as for *Chills*. Ask the vet to visit.

Lameness. Firstly, don't let a lame animal be ridden.

It is sometimes hard to make out on which side the donkey is lame, but remember that if the limp is in his front legs, he walks with his head nodding towards the sound side, and if in the back legs, the rump drops on the sound side.

Lameness can have various causes. It may arise simply from neglected and consequently mis-shapen feet, in which case you will have to call for a blacksmith's assistance. If you think the trouble is inside the hoof, clean it out gently with a hoof pick or pointed stick and see whether perhaps a thorn or nail is sticking into the frog. (Illustration on page 56). If so, after carefully working it out so as not to leave the point behind, put the foot in a disinfectant solution and, if the ground is wet, apply a little Stockholm tar all over the underside of the hoof.

Apart from the causes already mentioned, the two most common troubles behind lameness are laminitis and thrush, which are dealt with under separate headings.

Laminitis. This is inflamation of the sole of the foot and is very painful; it is usually caused by an excess of rich spring grass. If he is suffering from it, he will be lame and his hoof will feel very hot to the touch. Once contracted, the condition is liable to occur every spring unless stringent precautions are taken. These involve keeping the animal off grass during the day-time by shutting him in on a diet of hay. He can be given a bran mash — but without the addition of oats.

Prevention, with this complaint, is much easier than cure and it is usually only necessary to see that the donkey isn't suddenly introduced into an area of long rich spring grass. If he is living in his own field during the late winter and spring, he will keep pace with the season himself, so to speak. If it is necessary to introduce him into deep new pasture, it must be to a little at a time for about two or three weeks.

Lice. These pests, which fall into two categories — the biting and the sucking varieties — rank high among the ailments as a discomfort to an animal. They do not affect humans so there is no need to be cautious about investigating the donkey's coat. Some of these insects are small and hard to find, although their eggs are usually easy to spot —tiny whitish specks. The sign of lice infestation is the donkey biting himself and frequently rubbing against things. (Incidentally, rubbing doesn't necessarily mean lice, as he will rub himself to help loosen his thick winter coat, and, as previously stated, constant rubbing and biting can mean eczema). If untreated, lice will quite soon cause bare patches to appear in the animal's coat as a result of his scratching himself, so try not to let them get ahead of you to this extent. Incidentally, the ears are often the first part of the donkey to be affected.

Lice can be treated by applying various preparations, obtainable from your vet or some chemists. Beware of getting the powder into either your own or the donkey's eyes or nostrils. Choose a day that is neither windy nor wet (in the latter case the powder forms hard balls in the hair which are almost impossible to get out). The hair always takes a few weeks to grow again on the bare places, so don't panic if it seems to be taking a long time. Give the donkey a second powdering in two or three weeks after the first, as the lice eggs will have been unaffected by the treatment, but by this time will have hatched and may have escaped the effects of the powder residue in the coat. Concentrate the powder along the backbone and work it downwards by hand. (I recommend a pair of rubber gloves for this purpose, as the preparation smells pernicious and lasts for a long time).

Sometimes, with a neglected donkey, lice infestation can be so bad that clipping and singeing, or shampooing with a special shampoo obtainable from chemists, is the only answer. The shampoo, which contains an insecticide, must dry naturally and forms a sort of film over the animal's body. The shampooing has, therefore, to be done in warm weather or else he must be kept indoors for several hours afterwards until he is thoroughly dry.

Don't rub him dry or you will spoil the effect. The whole business is laborious and has to be repeated after ten days, so once again, save trouble for both yourself and the animal by paying a little attention to his toilet; in other words, give him a regular grooming and coat inspection.

Mastitis. This is not common but can be caused by a germ carried by flies or by dirty conditions, usually after a birth or following weaning. The symptoms are a painful, hot or over-swollen udder. Accumulated milk and septic matter may finally cause a puncture of the swollen udder or one of the teats. In the latter case, the teat is useless henceforward, but the place must be bathed morning and evening with salt water which should be fairly, but obviously not too, hot. Hold the wet cloth against the puncture until the septic matter and milk begins to trickle out — it usually takes five or six applications before this starts. Go on bathing it for ten minutes or a quarter of an hour. Do this every day until you can get no more matter out of the udder. The mare should be fed with two tablespoons of Epsom or Glauber salts mixed well into a bran mash twice a day while you are trying to reduce the milk flow. If you feed her this while you are attending to her affected parts, it will help to distract her.

If the foal has not been weaned and mastitis occurs, it is generally advisable to wean him forthwith if possible, or transfer him to a bottle, but your vet must advise you on this point. The mare should be fed on a rather limited quantity of hay throughout the course of the illness, and kept mainly off fresh grass; all of this helping to reduce the milk.

Treatment can be very difficult, depending on the mare's temperament. Should she be unfortunate enough to lose the use of one teat through puncture, do not despair of her being able to rear another foal. She can manage to do this tolerably well with only one side in working order, but naturally the utmost vigilance should be used to avoid a recurrence of the affliction with her next foal.

Pneumonia. If your donkey has a shelter and freedom to use it when he pleases, the danger of pneumonia is not great but it does exist. You will notice that he is ill by quick breathing, coughing, shivering, lack of appetite and generally wretched appearance. It can occur very suddenly, especially in foals, following a chill or cold if proper care has not been taken with these. Once pneumonia is contracted, you must of course treat the donkey under medical direction, keeping him as warm as possible indoors, although with plenty of fresh air. Feed him on the ground (see under Chills). It should be emphasised that pneumonia in a donkey is very serious indeed.

Ringworm. Should not be confused with other worm troubles, as it is a disease of the skin. It is infectious and can be caught from cattle by rubbing against posts and other objects on which they have scratched themselves. It cannot easily be mistaken for anything else, as circles will develop in the animal's coat and the skin underneath will turn grey and scaly. Veterinary iodine sometimes works a home cure, but it is usually advisable to call in the vet to treat it.

Scouring. This is another name for diarrhoea. Always keep an eye on an animal that is scouring, particularly foals. It may mean very little or just that the foal is affected by something in its mother's milk. However, it can be a symptom and precursor of severe illness, such as enteritis. It can also indicate worms or over-rich feeding.

Sores. If the donkey gets a sore from any part of his tack rubbing him, the main thing to remember is not to expose that portion of him again to the offending piece of leather or buckle until the sore has completely healed. Wash the place well with a disinfectant or salt water. Sores are often caused by dirty and hard leather — the condition of the girths being particularly important. Remember to keep the leather soft by regular cleaning.

A fairly common kind of sore is one that occurs below the eyes in summer time, usually on dark-haired donkeys. The sores are caused by flies concentrating round the eyes, and the constant trickling of tears down the face from the eyes, attracting more flies, makes the donkey rub his face on his legs until very soon red sores appear which can grow to several inches long; they are very tender and extremely unsightly. This is one reason why it is so important to provide shelter during the summer months. You can use an aerosol fly spray to deter the pests, but it needs to be done once a day if not more often during hot weather. Usually donkeys are frightened by the noise of the squirting, and it is hard to apply — one must be careful also not to aim into the eye itself. It is easier to apply some fly-repelling and healing ointment, but the irritation of the sore often causes him to rub this off within half an hour of the application. Apart from a shelter, a home-made fringe to hang over the eyes of badly affected donkeys during the hot time of the day, seems the best preventative. Attach the fringe to a headstall, taking off any dangling leading rein or rope. If it has a brow band, sew your fringe to it. and if not, you will have to improvise one. The fringe is quite easy to make and only takes a little

time. You can use whatever you think most suitable, either tough string or strips of plastic or leather. It should be several inches deep and each strip should be knotted at the bottom to keep it hanging down over the eyes. The strips should be close enough to be effective but not so close as to prevent the donkey from seeing, and should look something like the drawing on this page. The constant movement and brushing of the strips will keep away the flies. (One does not often see a donkey that suffers so badly as to warrant this, but they do exist, and once the trouble has really started, it is hard to clear up the sores until the summer is over).

Strangles. Highly infectious and contagious. Begins with streaming nostrils, and then a lump starts to develop between the jaw bones. The vet must be called and will probably give a course of injections, but the home treatment is most important. The swelling or lump must be bathed with hot salt water two or three times a day in order to bring it to a head and make it burst. If it bursts internally, the poison goes into the animal's system and is very dangerous. Once it has burst, go on bathing it with salt and water until it is quite clean and begins to heal. The whole course of the illness lasts for six weeks and the incubation period goes on for three weeks, so it is certainly a disease of which to beware. Once contracted, however, the donkey cannot catch it again.

All straw bedding used by the donkey must be burnt and the stable thoroughly washed — walls and all — with a strong disinfectant solution before any other equine is allowed to use it.

Sweet Itch. This is not common but is a most unpleasant affliction, believed to be caused by some food plant to which the animal is allergic. It can be described as an extreme form of eczema but it only affects the area of the mane and spine. Once contracted, it always recurs in warm weather or if the donkey is living on too rich a diet. It appears to be almost unbearably 'itchy', and the beast does

'Salt for the wit'

'Well, you might have waited!'

Supplementary menu

Growing up

everything it can to bite and rub the affected parts, including frequent rolling. There is no complete cure although the vet can alleviate it.

Thrush. This is a complaint very easily detected as it has a dreadful smell. It makes the animal lame and is caused by standing too much on muddy or very wet ground. The best means of prevention is to keep the donkey on as dry a footing as possible, and if impossible in winter, clean out his feet regularly with a hoof-pick. Thrush affects the frog of the foot (see illustration in Chapter 6) which goes soft. The treatment is to clean out the hoof carefully, soak it for a few minutes in a pail of salt warm water, dry it, and then apply Stockholm tar which keeps out the damp, filling up the whole hoof cavity with it. A little salt can be added to the tar.

Warble Fly. These large droning flies cause great alarm among field animals and they will run in all directions to shake them off. The flies have striped bodies and look more fearsome than they are, as in fact they do not sting. Their habits are, however, deplorable. They lay their eggs, which though small are yellow and therefore easily spotted, on the animal's coat. When they hatch out into grubs they irritate; the animal licks them off, and as with the grubs of the bot fly, they are swallowed. Thereafter they spend months inside the host, and the following spring make their way to the outside world by the shortest route, in other words by burrowing through his skin. They lie

F

close to the surface along the animal's back, causing lumps which can again be seen or at any rate
felt without much difficulty. This complaint is not
common except in areas where there are many
store cattle and is not really difficult to deal with.
If the eggs are few, they can be picked off with
your fingers quite easily; if numerous, it is possible
to buy preparations which, when sponged on, kill
the eggs and the emerging grubs.

Warts. These usually occur in young animals
and are generally found round the mouth and
sometimes round the eyes. They may grow large
and unsightly but they nearly always disappear
of their own accord. Occasionally, these warts turn
out to be malignant growths, but there is no means
of knowing this unless either the animal is obviously in pain and off colour, or if after two or three
months the wart does not disappear and the vet
considers it advisable to have it removed and
analysed.

This operation was performed on one of our
donkeys — a Jenny aged about two years. Beginning with a small wart, she gradually developed
a large and unsightly growth at the corner of her
mouth, about the circumference of a penny with
a red top to it. She did not appear to suffer from it
or to be off form in any way, but as after three
months the growth was still there, we consulted
our vet who decided to give her a general anaes-
ethic and cut it out. The lurid-looking object was
packed up and sent off to be examined, the vet

remarking that it would gladden the heart of some research worker! It turned out to be non-malignant. The donkey subsequently developed a small wart in the same spot, but this time it attained only decent proportions.

Worms. Worms are probably the chief source of trouble in donkeys. The main thing here is to keep on top of the situation by regular worming so that the stage is never reached when the animal's whole health is affected.

There are various kinds of worms which infect the horse breeds, but it is unnecessary to go into much detail as, broadly speaking, their effects are the same. Some are, however, much more serious than others. All donkeys have some worms, but they must be kept in check. They breed inside the host animal and their eggs pass out with the droppings and lie in the grass. Most remain alive up to six weeks but some species survive for months. The animal eats them again while grazing and the cycle is repeated. This is the main reason why it is inadvisable to keep a donkey in a very small area without change of grazing; six weeks of rest does much to clear a field of living worms or eggs. Sharp frosts will kill worm eggs lying on grass, so it is a good thing to rest the summer pasture during the winter months. Liming the field, also, is effective in killing the worms and eggs to a certain extent. In all cases it is a wise precaution to worm your donkey twice a year (usually spring and autumn), and where the pasturage is small it may be necessary to do it more often. As already suggested in Chapter 4, it helps if your paddock is big enough to divide in half so that the donkey can live for six weeks at a time in each.

The method of worming is quite simple nowadays; get the worm powder from your vet; measure out the quantity prescribed; make a small bran mash and mix the powder well in; and serve! There should be no difficulty at all in getting the donkey to eat this up quite cheerfully. If, however, the exceptional donkey suspects something and refuses his mash, you will have to drench him — in other words, forcibly pour a liquid mixture down his throat (as described at the beginning of this chapter). Do not let the donkey be much exercised for two days after worming.

If you are getting a new donkey and don't know where it has come from or how well looked after it has been, it is a good plan to worm it before putting it into its new quarters, and then again a fortnight later, so as to catch the second crop of worms that were in the egg stage for the first worming; and start with as clean a bill of health as possible. This doesn't mean that the animal will thereafter be free from worms — there are always some that escape and subsequently breed — and you should still give him a dose twice a year.

Donkeys pick up worms from each other of course — in particular, an older animal whose system has acquired a tolerance to them may carry a great many without too much effect on its health, but the eggs passed out will affect any young animal.

The main sign of bad worm infestation is listlessness, a hanging head, dull coat, dull eye and general inertia, slight at first, but getting steadily worse. The animal may look very thin and poor or it may have, deceptively to an inexperienced eye, a pot belly. Sometimes it will spend a great deal of time rubbing its backside against a post or something similar, or a yellowish discharge can be seen. A persistent cough may be a sign of lungworms; this is a most unfortunate stage to reach because if the lungs become badly damaged, this is permanent. The donkey can regain health after treatment but will blow heavily when moving fast. With a bad state of lung worms, you can hear a kind of subdued rattle with the intake of breath if you put your ear to the animal's chest.

Sometimes you can find worms in the donkey's droppings yourself, although this isn't always the case as some of the species are very small. Should you suspect infestation, your vet will have a sample of the droppings examined for you. To give you an idea of the relative size of worms: some knows as ascarids are up to a foot in length, while others, and amongst them the most dangerous, i.e. some of the strongyles, are under half an inch long.

Wounds. Never poke about in a wound to try and find whatever may have caused it if it isn't immediately apparent. Wash it with clean water, preferably gently squirted from a hose pipe and kept up for three or four minutes. Then bathe it with antiseptic lotion or salt and water. It must be kept clean and therefore it may be necessary to keep the donkey indoors on clean bedding until it has healed. It should, of course, be kept free of flies by using some ointment such as zinc, or one of the new sprays which can be prescribed by a vet, to give it a protective cover. Most common causes of wounds are wire, nails, sharp stick or stake wounds, and thorns. Blackthorn in particular can cause a poisonous wound.

Always consult the vet as to whether stitches are necessary if the wound is a large or nasty one.

Medicine Chest

There are a few basic things which it is always useful to have on hand either from the point of view of medical treatment or for general usefulness. Most of them have been referred to in the course of this chapter.

Cotton wool
Dettol or T.C.P.
Epsom salts
Friar's Balsam
Glucose
Jeyes fluid or other strong disinfectant
Louse powder
Some healing ointment, preferably with a zinc oxide
   base and containing a fly repellant such as
   camphor or oil of eucalyptus.

Salt
Stockholm tar
Zinc ointment.

If you own a foal, it is wise to keep the following items:

Baby's bottle and teats	It is best to have one of the wide-necked plastic bottles with a ring to hold the teat securely in position. The hole in the teat will need to be enlarged.

Small rubber syringe or small empty medicine bottle.

If a foal has, for one reason or another, to be given a substitute for its mother's milk, the following receipe shows how the feed should be made up:

13 oz. cow's milk
3 oz. lime water (see below)
Heaped tablespoon glucose
Tablespoon Ribena

There are, incidentally, 20 fluid oz. to the pint.

Lime water is made by soaking 2 oz. of calcium hydroxide in two pints of cold water. It should be left to stand for twelve hours before being used. Calcium hydroxide takes a very long time to dissolve, so it is possible to go on adding cold water to the solution as you use it over a week or two.

The foal should be fed anything up to 8 oz. at a time, the quantity and the intervals between feeds depending on its age and whether it is having any supplement from its dam — you will need to go into this with your veterinary adviser.

CHAPTER NINE

Tack

This comprises halter, headstall, bridle and saddle.

HALTER

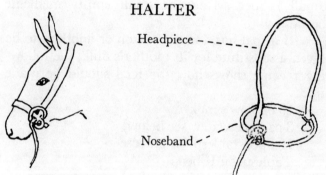

Halter with correct knot to prevent slipping

Halter with nothing to prevent rope pulling tight

The halter. The simplest pieces of equipment and the ones most often used are the halter and/or headstall. A halter should be made of webbing and is cheaper than a headstall. It is easy to slip on as follows:

Put the noseband over the donkey's nose and at the same time gently pull his ears through the head-piece. Adjust the tightness of the noseband and then take particular care that the rope attached to it is not pulling tight or tied by a slip knot, as the donkey can be half-stifled in this way if the noseband is worn too low. Make sure that a good firm knot prevents the rope from pulling tight. This is most important to remember when tethering or tying up the donkey. Incidentally, most pony halters are too big for a donkey, so you will have to take a tuck in the head-piece between the ears, or the nose band will come too low over the nostrils. Don't use safety pins for the purpose of this tuck, but sew it with thread.

HEADSTALL

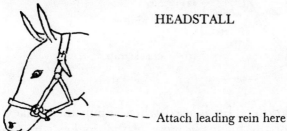

Attach leading rein here

The headstall is very useful as there is no risk of your tying a slip knot with the rope. It is really a kind of halter made of leather with a head-piece fastening with a buckle at the side. A rope or leading rein has to be attached at the point shown.

If you have a donkey that is hard to catch, such as a very new one, a headstall is invaluable as you can leave it on while the animal is loose in his field. It is easier to catch hold of this when you are trying to get him than to put a halter on him. However, if you do this, be sure not to leave a dangling rope attached that can catch in something and throw him or trip him up. Don't leave a headstall on him permanently as it will eventually rub and make a sore, but it is useful for temporary periods. (Incidentally, a dog lead makes a good substitute for a leading rein or rope).

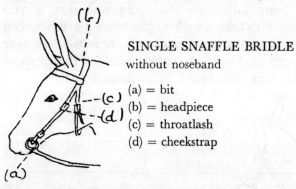

SINGLE SNAFFLE BRIDLE
without noseband

(a) = bit
(b) = headpiece
(c) = throatlash
(d) = cheekstrap

The bridle. This is used when riding the donkey. Present the bit (a) in front of the donkey's mouth with your left hand and gently but firmly press it between his lips, with the other hand pulling the head-piece (b) over his ears. He should then accept

the bit himself. Then buckle the throat lash (c)
on the near side (i.e. the donkey's left side), making
it neither too tight nor too loose. You will find
that there are also buckles on the cheekstraps (d)
which can be adjusted if necessary. Do not have
them too tight or they will raise the bit so that it
is cutting into the corners of the donkey's mouth,
but if they are too loose, the bit will be hanging
in the mouth and not controlling the animal at all.
Always use either a plain-jointed or half-moon
snaffle bit. They are the kindest bits, especially
with an inexperienced rider, and look like this:-

Half moon snaffle bit

Plain-jointed snaffle bit

The bridle illustrated is the simplest kind. Many
have a noseband and this is preferable if the rider
is very young or inclined to hold on by the reins, as
it takes some of the pressure from the mouth.

Don't use any old bridle you find up in the
loft; the bit may be cruel and the leather rotten.

The saddle. It is best to use a felt pad or numnah
saddle on a donkey. These often have a handle (a)
in front which is useful for small children and
prevents them holding on by the reins for balance.
This handle should be made of leather. A metal
handle could injure a child if he was thrown forward. When saddling, don't ruffle the hair the
wrong way.

Make sure that the saddle is fitted with the

proper stirrup bars (c) for young children. These enable the whole stirrup leather (e) to slip off easily if the child falls. There is another kind of bar

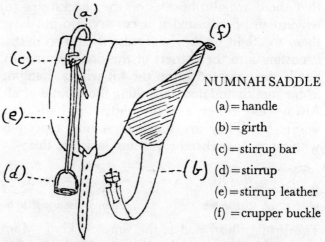

NUMNAH SADDLE

(a) = handle

(b) = girth

(c) = stirrup bar

(d) = stirrup

(e) = stirrup leather

(f) = crupper buckle

which turns up to prevent the leathers slipping off; this, especially if coupled with a stirrup that is too small, can be very dangerous should the child fall off and his foot remain caught in the stirrup. The stirrups (d) should be wide enough to enable the foot to slip in and out easily, although not too wide — there should be about an inch of play in them apart from the width of the foot.

When doing up the girths (b), which can be made of various materials, the best probably being either leather or lampwick, make sure that they are not twisted. You can do them up quite tight, as most ponies and donkeys blow themselves out while you are saddling them. The girths nearly always need to be tightened another couple of holes after the donkey has been ridden for a few minutes.

If you use a crupper, which is a strap with a loop for the tail, attach it to the saddle by the buckle (f). Slip the tail through the crupper before attaching it to the saddle, or else loosen the crupper buckle (f) so that it can be extended to go comfortably over the tail and re-buckled afterwards. Don't be lazy and saddle the animal with the crupper attached and buckled in the 'on' position and then twist the donkey's tail in order to get the loop of the crupper over it.

A crupper is not really necessary except with a very fat animal when the saddle may ease round however tightly you think you have done up the girths.

Keep all leather tack supple by regular cleaning and softening with saddle soap. A broken rein is a common cause of accident. Wash leather in tepid water, dry with a chamois leather and rub in saddle soap. 'Koachalin' rubbed in liberally is excellent if the tack is not to be used for some time. Undo any buckles when cleaning; otherwise the leather will crack at these spots because they will never be properly cleaned. 'Neatsfoot' oil is good but should be kept away from stitching, as it rots it.

Keep bits clean — they should always be thoroughly wiped after use. Wash them at regular intervals, clean them with metal polish, and shine. Stirrups should be treated in the same way.

Keep a felt saddle clean simply by brushing, and remember to beware of moth if it is stored away.

Tack should be hung up in a dry place as it can easily become mildewy. The saddle should be placed in the riding position on a stout peg or even on the back of an old kitchen chair. Never put a damp saddle on an animal's back.

CHAPTER TEN

Riding a donkey

IT IS important to remember that a donkey must not be ridden before a certain age or his back will be injured. A well-grown animal could have a small child lifted on to its back just to get the feel of it at eighteen months, but it must not be ridden about. At two years old you can begin to ride him gently, but a lot of trotting up and down should not be allowed until he is at least two and a half. Although a donkey is capable of carrying a great weight, it is not considered fair in this country to make him carry more than eight stone for other than very short distances, and then only at a walk. When you see donkeys carrying huge loads abroad, observe that it is most often carefully balanced and hung on each side of the animal, although many of us have had our indignation roused by seeing a very heavy man atop of them and perhaps a load as well.

Once a Jenny or gelding is old enough to be ridden, a child is usually safe on its back even though it may not have been what is known as "broken in", but an adult should hold the donkey's head the first time — just in case! This willingness to be mounted is a wonderful quality when one thinks of what can be involved in backing a horse for the first time. When first mounted a donkey will generally stand still or perhaps move about a little rather uneasily. After a minute or two, if he is already trained to follow he will be prepared to walk along with a child on his back quite peaceably if you lead him. This amenability, however, is not always to the poor donkey's advantage. People tend to put a bit in his mouth without more ado and no one bothers to teach him the most elementary aids. (Aids mean signals of instruction from rider to mount). If he has never had a bit in his mouth before, break him to it gently; let him wear it without a rider first for a few days — just slipping the bridle off and on. Never give a very small child a bit to hang on to unless you are there to supervise, or the donkey's mouth will be ruined very quickly; the reins are not designed as handles. With a very young child riding on his own, attach the reins to the noseband and if possible use a numnah saddle (with a handle in front to hold). Failing the latter, tell him to hold on to the mane for extra security.

It is sensible to teach children the basic rules of horsemanship at an early stage:

Mounting. Mount the donkey from the near side (left side). Gather the reins in the left hand firmly but not too tightly, throw the loose end over the donkey's neck to the off side, and with the same hand hold the front of the saddle. Face the tail, put your left foot in the stirrup, transfer your weight to that foot, and turning your body as you do so, throw your leg over.

Dismounting. You should dismount to the near side. Keep hold of the reins in your left hand, slip your right foot out of the stirrup, lean forward, press down on to the saddle with both hands, and pass your right leg over the donkey's back and down on to the ground. Then slip your left foot from the stirrup; do not give up the reins until you are standing firmly on the ground.

Aids.   If you want the donkey to turn to the right, you must slightly shorten the right rein and squeeze with your left leg; if you want him to turn left, vice versa. When you want him to move off from a standing position or to quicken his pace nudge him with your heels and say "Gee-up"; to stop him, pull gently on the reins using the word "Whoa".

The reins.   You should never hold on by the reins, but learn to keep your balance by the grip of your legs, and, if necessary, a steadying hand on the donkey's mane. To keep your balance by the reins hurts your mount's mouth: they are there for the rider to guide his mount, to check him and to show him who is in control.

Commands. As already said, the words "Whoa" and "Gee-up" should be used whenever necessary. It is a good thing to make sure that the donkey understands one or two other spoken words: "Stand" is a useful one, also "Steady", meaning, 'slow down' or 'careful'. "Ah" means he has done something wrong.

Trotting. If you are riding with a saddle at the trot, you should rise in the stirrups at every other pace — this rising and sitting rhythm comes quite naturally once you try it and is far more comfortable than bumping up and down.

Care. If your donkey has been working hard, e.g. trotting and cantering about for an hour or two with various children on his back, don't just run off and leave him at the end. After taking off his saddle (or even if he has not had one on), give him a good rubbing down. A titbit is usually appreciated at this stage and is well earned.

Respect. Children should be taught never to walk immediately behind a donkey. In fact, they rarely kick out at a child, but it is just as well to get him into the habit so that he is not over-familiar with ponies and horses at a later age.

Titbits. A reward after a good ride is always helpful towards a good relationship between mount and rider. The carrot, crust or whatever it is must always be held on the flat of the palm so that the donkey can take it easily between his soft lips. It is asking for trouble to hold the titbit between the fingers, as it is hard for the animal to see which is which, and a bitten finger is often the result.

Incidentally, titbits can be overdone as a reward. I remember seeing two small children mounted on fat ponies at a riding school. As they completed each circuit of the sawdust ring, the ponies came into the centre and nothing would make them budge until the master gave them sugar. There was not much doubt as to who had the whip hand in that case.

CHAPTER ELEVEN
Donkey and trap

In case you have the room and the wherewithal to enjoy this form of transport, I must put in a few words about it. First let me say that no one should drive on our modern roads without first being absolutely confident that he can master his equipage. Main roads are thoroughly dangerous to animals in harness unless handled by an expert, and by-roads, which are so often twisting and narrow, are just as risky. Very good fun can be had from a cart in fields, but of course the site has to be suitable, not too hilly nor waterlogged, and the cart should have pneumatic tyres.

Secondly, don't attempt to drive at night or

at dusk — even with proper lamps. Cars don't expect to meet anything of the size of a donkey and trap to be moving so comparatively slowly, and there is no need to elaborate on the kind of accident which could arise to either party from your taking a risk of this kind.

Thirdly, I must add that the harness should be a proper fit on the donkey or you will be very unfair to him. Don't try to get away with using something that was intended for a bigger animal. Harness has been evolved over the years to provide the right balance between pony (or donkey) and cart and to help the former whenever the nature of the ground becomes difficult. For instance, the action of the breeching is designed to keep the cart back when the animal is going downhill; if the breeching is too big, there is nothing to stop the cart banging on to his rear, which frightens him as well as placing undue strain, and can cause an accident. Apart from reasons like this, there is the more obvious effect of sores and galls caused by ill-fitting harness.

Traps and harness for donkeys are not so easy to come by, but you do occasionally see them advertised or coming up for auction at a horse-. fair. The most common trap to be seen is a governess cart (so called because governesses used to drive their charges in a tub vehicle of this kind). These carts are safe in so far as it is not easy to fall out of them — however, there is also the consideration that they are not so easy to evacuate in a hurry.

If you are completely inexperienced, try and get someone who knows about them to help you look trap and harness over and fit the harness for the first time.

The diagram shows a donkey wearing trap

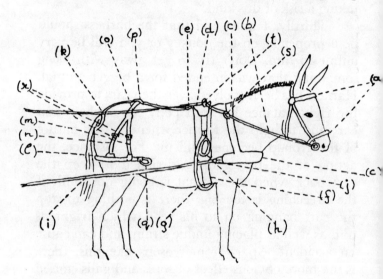

(a) Bridle
(b) Long reins
(c) Collar and breast-piece of collar
(d) Pad
(e) Buckle of pad
(f) Girth
(g) Balancing strap or belly-band
(h) Tugs
(i) Traces
(j) Hames clip

(k) Crupper
(l) Breeching
(m) Loin strap
(n) Quarter strap
(o) Cross strap
(p) Loop in crupper strap
(q) Buckle on breeching strap
(r) Buckles of loin strap and quarter strap
(s) Rein ring on collar
(t) Rein terret or pad ring

harness, and each piece is labelled for easy reference. (There are variations in harness, but to describe one type should help you to understand the principle).

Harness should be put on in the following order: either have the donkey haltered or else put on the bridle (a) having first unbuckled the long reins (b) or tied them up into bunches well out of the way; (the bridle can be put on last of all). Then put the collar (c) over the donkey's head. The collar in the illustration is what is known as an American collar — with a broad and padded piece going across the donkey's breast. The other

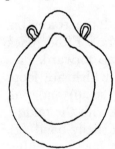

type of collar is perhaps more familiar; it is rather heavy and padded all round and you pass it over the donkey's head upside down, i.e. with the pointed end down, and once over the ears turn it round to its right position. Not all donkeys' heads will go through the appropriately-sized collar and I recommend the American collar for preference when driving them.

Next put on the pad (d) with the buckle (e) pointing towards the tail, as if it were an ordinary saddle, and do up the girth (f) (the further forward of the two bands). Leave the balancing strap or belly-band (g) undone until the shafts are through the tugs (h).

The traces (i) must be attached to the collar

at the hames clip (j) and you can either do this now, knotting them up out of the way, or at the next stage but one.

The crupper (k) and breeching (l) are usually put on all in one piece and this is the next thing to fit. The breeching is held in place by the loin strap (m) and quarter strap (n) which join in the cross strap (o). This threads the crupper strap at (p). Lay the whole thing across the donkey's back and pull it towards and over the tail, so that the breeching encircles the hindquarters. Gently push the tail right through the crupper. Next buckle the other end of the crupper strap to the pad buckle (e), adjusting it later if necessary.

With all this completed and the traces on, your next task is to attach the trap. Either back the donkey into it or pull the trap forward. Pass the shafts through the tugs (h) (which are loops on the belly band or balancing strap) and pull them forward until they are level with the middle of the shoulder; then fasten the belly-band (g). Next attach the traces (i) to the hooks at either side of the front of the trap. You will find that the buckle (q) on the breeching strap is opposite a hook on the inside of the shafts. Buckle the breeching strap through these hooks. You may have to adjust the height of the breeching by adjusting the buckles at the points marked (r). It should lie across the donkey's hind-quarters just below the level of the shaft.

Now buckle the long reins on to the bridle

(or untie them) and if they are buckled together at what can be described as the trap end, undo them and pass them through the rings (s) on the top of the collar and (t) on the pad and then buckle them together again. (This process can be reversed, of course, ending up with buckling the reins on to the bridle).

Your equipage should now be complete.

A donkey coming from Ireland is often used to being driven, but you can never be certain until you try him out. He may back easily into the shafts and from that point you can soon see how used he is to a trap. If he is obviously afraid, you will have to train him carefully yourself. This is a job which calls for patience and gentle handling. Do not attempt to put him in the trap until he is thoroughly accustomed to the harness. Let him wear it on several occasions and walk him about to give him the feel of it. It doesn't matter if various straps and things are left dangling, so long as they are not trailing on the ground so as to trip him. A bit of jingling at this stage will accustom him to more later on. The next step is to get two people to hang on to the traces while you lead him, so that he gets the feeling of pulling something (page 104). Now attach the traces to the breeching and let them pull from in front. This causes the breeching to pull tight against his hindquarters in the same way as it would if it were taking the strain of the trap going downhill.

Next teach him to be driven by walking behind with the long reins. You will need a light whip to tell him when to go forward at first as well as a firm "Gee-up".

Now at last you can try him in the trap. You can use a blinkered bridle so that he cannot see the wheels coming behind him, but this is rarely necessary. At first lead him and then practise driving him while walking beside or behind the trap, using the long reins as though you were in it. Finally, get into the trap, with the knowledge that by now he knows thoroughly what to expect.

Emphasis must be placed on the importance of getting the donkey used to all the rattle and jingle of the harness before he actually comes to take the weight of the trap. Otherwise he will certainly be frightened and probably bolt when he finally feels it behind him.

I had a most alarming experience some years ago. I put a new but sober donkey into a governess cart and she blinked not an eye but rather appeared to consider it a common occurrence. So much so, that I skipped trying her out with the long reins before getting into the trap myself, and let six children take her off along the drive. Almost at once she bolted, and with the trap swaying wildly, galloped straight for a pond, swerved at the last moment and came to rest beside the gate into her field. The children were delighted but I felt most conscience-stricken, imagining how much to blame I would have been if the trap had overturned.

CHAPTER TWELVE

The obstinate donkey

UNQUESTIONABLY donkeys can be obstinate, but the thing to remember is that they are not necessarily so and can be as easy to lead about and handle as any other animal. They are the most patient beasts and immensely willing, and those who have seen them working abroad, or, for that matter, even on our own beaches, will have no doubts that they are biddable. It is simply a quest-ion of perseverance in training — combining kind-ness with firmness.

Donkeys do undoubtedly come in for knocks; if you don't know your animal's past history and you find him difficult, it is probably because he has been frightened as a youngster. Several don-keys that have come to us have been highly nerv-ous and adamant about refusing to go places! In the end patience and psychology have made them manageable. By psychology I don't mean the traditional carrot dangled at the end of a stick. This rarely works, and in any case, as I have already said, over-feeding with titbits is one sure way of spoiling the animal, quite apart from the fact that you don't want to have your pockets permanently full of crumbs and apple peel. The best psychology is to try and borrow another don-key or pony of sober behaviour and get someone to lead it along in front of the difficult one, which you take yourself. It will invariably follow and will thus get into the way of being led.

Remember that although you are unlucky if you get a really obstinate donkey, it is nearly always possible to remedy this failing in the end. A final point: to lose your temper does absolutely no good at all — it may exhaust you but will make no difference whatsoever to the moke. Obstinacy often

arises from nervousness, and this has to be overcome before you can get anywhere.

The other practical thing to remember is that the correct way to lead a donkey is from the near side with your right hand at his head, so that if necessary you can reach back your left arm and give him a tap behind with a switch.

Either lead with an attached leading rein or hold the reins together in your right hand just behind his chin; never lug him along pulling one rein from the side or front, or the bit will hurt his mouth.

The only way to gain the confidence of a frightened animal is persistence in talking to it quietly and in approaching it without bustle or hurry. Don't despair if you buy an apparently tractable donkey at a fair and, after turning it loose in its paddock, find that you can't get near it. This has happened to us two or three times. I will quote an extreme case: we bought a one-year old Jenny at a horsefair and at the end of two months we had not got within ten yards of her, although at first the distance between us was much greater. We persevered, always talking to her, trying to approach her once or twice a day, and slowly the distance decreased. At last the day came when, standing about five or six feet away, my husband held out a titbit as usual with his arm extended to its limit, and the donkey stretched out her neck and, very tentatively indeed, made contact. It still took a week or two before she would accept a titbit without suspicion or before she would allow her neck to be stroked but thereafter her confidence increased very rapidly. We have now had this Jenny for a couple of years and she is one of the most affectionate animals we own, although rather nervous of strangers. But no one could guess from her present demeanour what a terrified young filly she was.

Sometimes in a case of this kind you will find that you can touch the donkey more easily if you approach from behind, although of course this is really against the rules. It is important to remember to make sure that he knows you are there. A nervous animal is often more chary of its head being touched than any other part and consequently swings round so that its hindquarters are confronting you. This doesn't mean that it is necessarily going to kick, but it is a position of defence. Approach obliquely from behind, talking quietly, and see if he will let you touch his rump or back. Stroke him gently, and if all goes well, gradually move your hand up his body until you reach his neck and eventually are in a position to tickle him behind his ears, which he loves! Donkeys practically always show when they are about to kick deliberately by laying back their ears and at the same time swishing their tails rather in the manner of an aggravated cat. They will also give an occasional quick sideways kick if irritated by a dog or something of this kind.

The three key things to remember when trying to approach a frightened animal are (1) no sudden or loud noises, (2) no sudden movements and (3) that the human voice is for some reason reassuring; so talk quietly to it.

Lastly — if you are desperately trying to move a really stubborn donkey from A to B in a hurry, pushing is invariably more effective than pulling!

CHAPTER THIRTEEN

Having a foal

DONKEY foals are irresistible. Under a toy animal's furry coat they combine a sturdy independence with at first great gentleness and later a most attractive impudence. They take a long time to arrive in the world — longer even than a pony foal, the average gestation period of a Jenny donkey being twelve and a half months, although there are occasional surprises at eleven and a half months.

So if you own a Jenny and decide to let her have a foal, lay your plans a year ahead so as not to clash with your holiday away. From the donkey's point of view, of course, spring and summer is the best time of year for a foal, but autumn and winter babies grow thick woolly coats very quickly and usually thrive.

A Jenny comes into season roughly every three weeks and the period lasts about seven days. With most Jennies this happens all the year round, barring December and January, but there are always exceptions. Some of them seem to go off season for a bit longer, and we have had a donkey in season in December. Although young Jennies may start coming into season before the age of two, they should not be allowed to be served by a stallion until they are two years old at least.

Having decided to embark upon a donkey family, you will have to find a donkey stallion and pay a stud fee. Your Jenny will either have to be taken to him or he will have to visit you, according to whatever arrangement you come to with his owner. Unfortunately, it is hard, if not impossible, to tell when a donkey is in season if she lives on her own. This may be important to know because there will be all the difference in the world in her treatment by some stallions if she is willing to stand for him (i.e., is in season) or if she will have none of him. In the latter case, some stallions can be very rough indeed and inflict severe bites; they may be perfectly quiet with humans but yet be a real nuisance and affliction to a modest Jenny donkey with whom they are not yet well acquainted. Incidentally, once a stallion has served a Jenny over her season, she counts as belonging to him and will not be molested roughly again.

If your Jenny lives with another donkey mare or a gelding, they may mount her at this time, but otherwise the only way to tell whether she is in season is to observe closely her behaviour when introduced to the stallion, as if the time is right she will always show the same sign. This is a rhythmic opening and shutting of her mouth when she is approached by the stallion. Once seen, it is quite unmistakable.

Not all stallions are forward; our gentle Koko, already referred to, was sometimes very diffident on nuptial occasions and took some time to take the plunge. Our present stallion, who is usually master of any situation without being rough, was on one occasion observed cantering round a field being chased by an ardent Jenny.

If the stallion is a rough customer, and if practicable, it pays to introduce the donkey couple across a gate or fence, and if the characteristic sign is wanting, try again two or three days later, and so on. It is usually considered wise to leave the Jenny with the stallion until her next season is due after she has been covered, i.e. for another month, to be on the safe side and make sure that she is in foal.

After this there is nothing to do but wait. The mother-to-be needs no special treatment except that she can do with extra rations in the winter or if her grazing is limited, and it is kinder not to ride her hard in the last month or two. As her time draws near, you can again find a sign which will give you an indication of 'when'. Her udder will begin to distend about a month before the foal is born and will become really swollen a week before. Don't fuss around her too much; some donkeys really seem to object to being peeped at continually and appear to wait to give birth until you're not there. They like to produce their foals in the open and to choose their own spot, tending to become agitated if they are shut in; so don't interfere by doing this unless the weather is especially cold or wet.

The birth itself should be simple and over in about half an hour or less, the foal being presented with head and front legs first. If the Jenny seems to be having difficulty and takes over half an hour, call your vet at once but don't attempt to help her yourself unless you have previous experience, as you can do great damage to both mare and foal. After the birth she likes to clean the foal and rest a little without interruption. She may really resent your premature appearance, especially if it is her first foal. Usually I make the mother a warm mash and take it to her an hour or so afterwards. Use a little tact and pet her first before trying to make her baby's acquaintance. Always check to find the afterbirth, which should, incidentally, be buried so as to discourage flies, as failure to produce this within a few hours of the birth can be very dangerous for the mare. If you are sure that she has not cleansed, send for your vet.

Don't be worried if you find pieces of rubber-like substance lying near the place where the foal was dropped. The foal's hooves are sheathed in this to protect the mother from injury at the time of birth. It comes away naturally from the hooves in about half an hour or so.

Very occasionally indeed a mare will not take to her foal. This happened to us with an older Jenny who produced her foal about a week prematurely. It was a very small and helpless creature, perfectly formed except for its feet which looked as if they hadn't been finished off quite neatly. We found it lying on the grass, quite untouched by its mother, trying gamely to struggle to its feet without success. The mother was lying down some way from it, but got up after a while and wandered over to it. She looked at it rather closely for a minute and then deliberately turned her back and wandered off to graze in another part of the field. Because he seemed in such poor shape I roughly dried the foal's coat with a towel, this stimulus normally being given by the mother's tongue, and we helped him to his feet; he was very wobbly but made plucky attempts to walk about. Nothing, however, would induce the mother to allow him to suckle from her, although she was tied up and

H

firmly held while the foal was put to her. She fought hard and very little milk went down the baby's throat. The colostrum, or first milk, which is yielded by the mare at this time, is important for the health of the foal, but she was quite unmanageable. Too late, we tried to bottle feed the baby, but it was so discouraged that it would not suck and our standard method of feeding in difficult cases with a little rubber syringe didn't work very well, as it struggled not to swallow. Minute quantities went down but the rest just trickled out of the side of its mouth. Although my husband remained with the foal all night trying to feed it, his efforts were of no avail and the poor thing died the following day. It was that particular mare's third foal since we had had her. She had been an excellent mother on both other occasions and her foals had thrived. We wondered whether she rejected this one simply from shock because it was premature and thus caused its death, or whether she knew that it was likely to die and therefore did not bother with it.

Salt sprinkled onto the foal's coat will sometimes induce an uninterested mare to start licking, but unfortunately we didn't know this at the time. Not all mares show an immediate interest in their foals in any case. Don't panic if, even after she has cleaned it, she pushes it away from her for a little while. If you leave her alone for a couple of hours with the baby, she will get used to the idea and soon they will be inseparable.

The Jenny will come in season again about a week after foaling. There seems no particular reason why a healthy donkey should not be covered again immediately, but we prefer to give our Jennies a rest of several months between pregnancies; after all, they are feeding a foal and it seems rather hard to put a double drain on their resources year after year.

I have often been asked whether it is safe to leave the donkey stallion in the field with the Jenny at the time of and after foaling. From our own experience I can say "Yes" without qualification. The stallion usually shows some interest in the foal immediately after birth, but the mother will not let him come very close as a rule. Later on when she allows it, our stallions and foals have always become good friends. I always remember a very hot day in summer when all the donkeys were sheltering from the sun and flies in their stalls. At about midday our big twelve-hand stallion emerged, obviously feeling rather bored, and, followed by one of the foals aged about two months, he went off to the dust bath in the middle of the field where he proceeded to have a good roll. As soon as he had finished, Sambo, the foal, followed his example. The pair then started off at a gallop for the sheds as if racing, and whisked indoors. It was unusual for a foal to leave its mother's side when so young.

Of course, there comes a stage when the stallion may begin to resent the presence of another male in his herd; we take away the young colts at about eight to ten months. On one occasion we isolated a stallion and a colt of about a year old, both of whom were suffering from strangles. They remained together quite happily for about six weeks to two months, probably because there were no Jennies in sight. However, when their quarantine period was over, we put them both into a field with some Jennies. The next day, the colt was found to have a large and unpleasantly suppurating wound in his ear caused by a bite. Although there was no direct evidence, it seemed certain that it must have been inflicted by the stallion, so we took no more chances and separated them.

All this is derived from our own experience only. An acquaintance with a fairly wide knowledge of donkey habits, told me of a newly born foal that had been severely bitten all over by a stallion. I have also heard from other sources that a stallion may resent a foal brought into his field with its mother, so that it seems wiser to let the birth take place there if this is possible to arrange rather than introducing the foal afterwards. On the whole, I should think that the entire question depends on the stallion's temperament; as I say, we ourselves have had no first-hand experience of trouble of this kind although stallions and foals have always mixed freely.

Stallions will often plague a filly of eighteen months or so before she begins coming into season, and it is as well to separate them at this time unless they are of an equal age and have been brought up together, so that she has no compunction about standing up for her rights, and is used to 'horse-play'. Otherwise he can make her quite miserable.

CHAPTER FOURTEEN

Care of foals

A YOUNG donkey is a delightful play-fellow for children. For your own future comfort, however, use a little discretion and draw certain limits to intimacy. For instance, don't produce titbits the whole time or encourage it to be quite at home in the kitchen; what is amusing in a small donkey can be very tiresome in a full-grown one. You don't want a full-sized donkey butting and pushing visitors unmercifully for something to eat out of their handbags and pockets.

The newly-born foal gets onto its feet very quickly, usually after a few minutes. It then wobbles about, learning to control its legs, and becomes master of the situation in an extraordinary short time. At this stage, if kept in a field with other donkeys, there usually follows an inspection of the new arrival, which most Jennies permit provided the friends and relations don't press in too closely. Foals are generally fearless when approached by people for the first time, although often by the second day some will have started a shy fit which is best overcome by feigning to ignore it while you talk to and fondle the mother. Inquisitiveness, always a guiding motive with donkeys, will soon gain the upper hand, and in two or three days' time the foal will be running to meet you.

Some Jennies will be a bit stand-offish for a week or two after producing their first foal. Don't follow them about or let children pester them, and they will gradually relax.

Thinking back over the many foals born here, two in particular come to mind. Both were the foals of Jennies that were very devoted to humans, and neither of them ever suffered anything resembling a shy period. One, whom we named M'Boyo, was the first donkey foal to be born on our premises; I knelt beside him as he stood staring at us, aged two or three hours old, and he promptly walked onto my lap where he stood clumsily balanced and then, quite unexpectedly, kicked me! The other, who is now our stallion, was born on a dark night in December. We went to check that his mother, whom we knew was "due", was all right, and found that he had arrived. He was so new that he decided that the pair of us plus a torch were more interesting than his own mother and persisted in trying to follow us. We finally made our escape, as far as I can remember, without the aid of the light, and left his mother to cope. A few hours later she would have resented this attachment on his part, but she was still resting after the birth and not taking a great deal of notice.

The foal has to learn to drink from its mother and strangely enough it has no instinct about which end of her to try! Almost invariably they seem to begin by pressing their noses behind her forelegs; even after they have found the right place several times by nosing down her length, they will still return to her forelegs. There is no need to worry about this, as they will sort themselves out; you can help them to get started, but it is not really necessary.

The daily needs of a foal are provided by its mother. From her it will learn about the all-important fact of earning its livelihood by grazing; it will start to nibble busily away at grass at a few weeks old. It should also learn from her when to seek shelter, although some Jennies are careless  about taking their foals indoors during snow or rain. The foal uses his mother as a butt for games of pushing, kicking and charging and usually she takes it all in good part, only occasionally giving him a sudden determined nip if she feels he is getting too obstreperous.

From the earliest age, when galloping or

cantering, the foal carries its head in the characteristic donkey way, holding it very high. The head
is sometimes held in this position, too, when he is
trotting with a somewhat high-stepping gait, although when older the trot becomes a much more
sober affair. Two donkey foals kept in the same
field provide hours of enjoyment for anyone with
time to watch them. They play great chasing
games, galloping wildly after each other in circles,
and then, on coming to grips, rear up, pushing each
other and intertwining their necks. Sometimes on
a warm summer evening when all the donkeys have

ventured out from sheltering from the flies, a horse-
fly or something else will frighten one of them, and
it will start to canter. Then the whole herd will
join in, and with the foals in the lead, career round
and round the field, quite obviously enjoying themselves enormously.

Foals are naturally lively and inquisitive, and
if you notice listlessness and lethargy, get your vet

to come at once. The sooner it has treatment the better, and this is a maxim for any complaint with any age of animal, but is even more applicable to a foal, as it hasn't the same reserves of strength as a grown animal. Specific signs which would indicate that there was something wrong with the youngster are an unusually swollen udder in the mare (showing that the foal is not drinking), or, in the foal, drooping ears, or ears which are either icy cold or burning hot to the touch. Scouring is always a danger sign (see page 78) and so is dehydration — easily detected by pinching the foal's skin; if it lies so close to the ribs that you cannot gather it at all between your fingers, this shows that it isn't having enough sustenance from its mother. It cannot be stressed too much that, should a foal not appear alert and gay, something is wrong and you should act at once in getting veterinary advice before it is too late.

If I had written this chapter after only a year or two's experience, I would have said that foals were on the whole tough little animals. Since then I have come to realise that we were lucky during our apprenticeship and that they cannot exactly be described as robust — at any rate in this country — and do need a careful eye kept on them when they are small. It may be worth recording here some troubles we have experienced with foals during the last two or three years.

Enteritis, usually brought on by a chill, seems to be the most deadly of the ailments which foals contract; pneumonia, which they can take very suddenly, is a close second. There are also mysterious complaints which defy analysis, such as the filly of about two to three months that suddenly began to wilt. We could see by her dam's udder that she wasn't suckling, and for the rest of the day no one could determine what was wrong, although she was obviously very weak. At last we found that the inside of her mouth was covered with marks rather resembling burst blisters, and it was plain that it was most painful to her when we touched her gums. Her mouth was in fact so tender that she couldn't bear the pain of suckling. We brought her in to a stall, gave her a deep strawy bed and kept her as warm as possible. On the vet's instructions we fed her every two or three hours with a milk preparation (see Chapter 8). (The mother's milk could have been used if we had had the time to milk her but it was a period of household crisis and we weren't able to do this as well. Fortunately she was a quiet donkey who let another foal suckle her two or three times a day, which relieved her — but not all Jennies will let another foal drink from them). We fed the foal by means of inserting a small rubber syringe at the side of its mouth and squeezing out the milk, a little at a time. At first she was so weak from lack of sustenance that she could scarcely stand, but after a day's supply she became much stronger and resisted the feeding, which made things more difficult. Fortunately after the next day the trouble

in her mouth began to subside, and on the fourth
day she was back with her mother and able to
drink naturally again. We have never found out
the cause of this strange affliction; presumably it
was caused by a plant — but what plant is still a
mystery, and nothing of the same kind has occured
since.

Trouble of a different kind was caused by a
filly born on Boxing Night. She evidently rolled
under a fence while struggling to get on her legs
after birth, and slithered partly down a slope into
a wood until caught by her fore-legs in a bit of
old netting wire. This happened at about mid-
night and it was pure luck that we had known her
mother was going to foal that night and were
therefore able to find her. We knew the Jenny's
time was imminent and went to give her a look-
over at about 11 p.m. Her behaviour made it plain
that the foal was on the way, so we retired and
came out again an hour later. However, on going
to peep at her we found her standing quietly in a
corner beside the after-birth but with no sign of
any offspring. It was her first foal and she seemed
quite bemused. The foal made no sound and was
lying quite out of sight, and only our desperate
probings with the torch into the surrounding black-
ness, revealed where she was lying. It was an extremely cold night and she would certainly have
been dead by the morning. My husband carried
her up to the stall but we didn't dare to rub her
dry as we longed to do as the mother showed little

interest in her. The mare's licking is the natural way of getting the baby's circulation going and it is thought that she licks because she likes the taste of the wet and sticky fur. If the baby is dried by other means, the mother has no incentive for licking and may lose interest in the foal altogether. The foal's legs were swollen where they had been caught, but she seemed in fairly good shape otherwise, so we left her alone with her rather uninterested mother with some trepidation. However, to our joy, on visiting her an hour later she was suckling. Because of the damaged knee muscles, she had to be kept in and for some time did not show signs of thriving. The weather turned very cold and I resorted to dressing her in a little woollen coat; this consisted of a small knitted blanket put across her back, fastened by a loop and button on her breast, again by a loop and button under her belly and finally held in place by a "crupper" of several strands of wool. The trouble with doing something like this in cold weather is that you have to keep it up. I didn't dare to take the coat off, even though the filly grew quite lively, until the weather became mild (plate at page 64). Even then, she had to be kept in at night until about the end of April or beginning of May, for fear of her taking cold. However, all subsequently went well. Another foal, born in December in an uneventful way, grew an extra thick woolly coat in a matter of a week or so and grew up without even a sniffle.

The case of Sambo was sadder. He was a

most affectionate and lively little animal with every appearance of robustness. He was six months old when the winter started and he quickly grew his thick coat in time for the severe weather. One day at the end of January, I noticed that he coughed a little and did not appear very lively. It was early days at our stud and I did not at that time realise the significance of lassitude, so it simply did not occur to me that disaster was round the corner. That night there came an extraordinary cold snap subsequently quoted as breaking some meteorological record. In the morning we found him lying in the stall and he died a few moments later. An autopsy showed complete congestion of the lungs — in other words acute pneumonia. Evidently he had had a bad cold — and although he had stayed indoors, the icy night air had been too much for him.

More recently we have had the case of a two-month-old foal which could not get enough nourishment from its mother. Although a sleek, plump and well-fed donkey, her milk began to dry up and her foal began to look droopy. Once again, it was not easy to establish what was wrong as there were no symptoms other than weakness and dehydration. When the cause was discovered, there was nothing for it but to supplement his diet with a bottle — at first every three hours, but as he became stronger we reduced it to four times a day; first thing in the morning, mid-day, 5 p.m., and last thing at night. We used the substitute for milk described in Chapter 8 (page 87).

There was no question of forcible-feeding in his case. Someone appeared in the field with the baby's bottle and M'Gee came straight for it! The number of feeds are being gradually reduced as he grows older, so that at six months he will be weaned from the bottle, although he may still be taking a little from his mother.

To sum up on the subject of mishaps and afflictions, I would say as a general rule with foals, take every precaution you can without going to the extreme of making them too soft. Always inspect them carefully after a very cold or wet night at any season of the year; if they seem listless and cold, bring them in and keep them in the stall until the weather improves. Never rub them dry; you will merely make the protective undercoat wet. Always follow up the slightest symptom and never hesitate to consult your vet.

Weaning should not be carried out unless absolutely necessary before the foal is six months old. There is no need to wean it then unless you want to for reasons of your own or unless the mare is again half way to her next foal, having been served after foaling. In fact, the longer a foal has the benefit of its mother's milk as a supplement to the regular grazing which it starts after four or five months, the better it does. At a year, it will have finished weaning itself and should be a beautifully strong little animal. Occasionally, a young donkey of over a year old will suckle every now and then or try to, but this does no harm.

If you do have to wean the foal before this, it should be done with care. Begin by accustoming the Jenny to losing her foal for a few hours at a time and let it return to her at night. Keep this up for a week or two if possible, and then for two or three days before the final separation keep the mare off grass and confine her to a not too plentiful diet of hay. Put a couple of tablespoonfuls of Epsom salts to each gallon of her drinking water as this will help to reduce her milk. Then, once you have taken the foal away, keep her in the same circumstances for three or four days, keeping an eye on her udder. Should it remain terribly swollen after two days, you can put the foal back to drain it off a bit, or better still, milk her a little yourself, but don't do this unless she is obviously in great distress as it tends to re-stimulate the flow of milk. If you do have to milk her, talk soothingly, press your head into her flank and gently but firmly squeeze the teats downwards with the thumb and first and second fingers. She may allow you to do this or she may not. It not, the vet can give her an injection to reduce the milk. (Incidentally, it is kind to give the Jenny the company of another animal if possible during this trying period).

The Jenny's bad time should not last for more than three days after the foal is taken right away.

Late autumn, winter and early spring are the best times for weaning from the point of view of the Jenny, as the grass is not so rich then — it is hard to be brought in from rich summer grass and kept entirely on hay. From the point of view of the foal, however, winter weaning, with the sudden loss of his mother's milk, will be more felt than in autumn and spring. So be sure to add to his diet of hay a small bran mash every day or whatever other food supplement your veterinary surgeon recommends. Remember also that he will need companionship and petting particularly at this time so that he doesn't miss his mother too much.

Once he is away from his mother, it is most important to keep him quite out of her sight and sound for a good three weeks and, if possible, longer. He must not be allowed to run with her until at least three months have passed or he may try to suckle again and re-induce the milk flow. Out of sight is out of temptation and it is kinder to the mare not to be able to see her foal at first.

Weaning is, of course, the best time to train a young donkey to lead, as he will just then be most dependent upon you and will probably be quite willing to follow. Put a halter on him occasionally for a few moments when he is a baby and you will overcome any nervousness he may have about ropes right from the start. At this age he is, of course, easier to handle if in an obstinate frame of mind, and a good push from behind will show him that you are boss. Remember to talk to him quietly all the time you are teaching him.

I must refer at this point to Chapter 10 about riding donkeys. It cannot be sufficiently stressed that no child, however light, should be lifted on to the back of a foal.

If your foal is a colt, the question of whether or not to have him gelded will arise sooner or later. Remember that if you want to keep him permanently and if he will be living with his mother, it would be unwise to let them breed, which would certainly result if he is not castrated.

Gelding should always be done by a vet. A colt can be castrated at the age of two or three weeks, and many people have the operation performed at this time. It is not however, always entirely satisfactory, as his testicles may not have developed evenly, and if he is cut in this condition he will grow up into what is known as a rig — in other words he is not clean-gelded and will later show some of the characteristics of a stallion; he may even be able to get a foal. After this early age, the testicles retract and the colt cannot be gelded until anything from the age of one year upwards: some mature much earlier than others. If the cutting is done at this time, a clean job is made of it and no mistakes should occur. It is important to have the operation performed in the spring or autumn: if it is done in the summer, there is danger of infection carried by flies, and if in the winter, there is the risk of a chill.

Many vets now believe in giving the animal a general anaesthetic. One cannot help feeling that this is much the kindest way. However effective a local anaesthetic may be, the animal still has

I

the use of its senses and will naturally be frightened by what is going on. So many gelded donkeys are nervous of men that one deduces it is fear left over from this experience.

Of course not all who perform the operation are particular about the pain and fright caused to the animal. Have a colt gelded before you sell him unless he is going to a home which specifically wants a stallion, otherwise there is no knowing how he will be treated. Not many people do want a stallion unless it is for breeding purposes, so it is safer to do what you can to assure him a good home by gelding him young and under your own supervision.

CHAPTER FIFTEEN

The mind of a donkey

Donkeys, although their faces may belie it, are almost all endowed with a sense of humour, sometimes mischevious but rarely malevolent; and all, without exception, have definite character-istics of their own. In our establishment, which has ranged up to nearly twenty donkeys, I can recall some trait peculiar to every animal. The specialist in practical jokes is MeMoke, the "Wit" illustrated at page 80 and our "Head Donkey", as visiting children call her. She really is the head donkey, as most of the others follow her example in matters of daily life, choosing which part of their range they will graze in the morning, coming to the gate to stare hopefully at the house, and lining up for hay rations. As I have said, MeMoke has an original turn of mind which was first demonstrated when we had had her only a short time. My husband was talking to her across a barbed wire fence when suddenly she leaned over and took his tie firmly between her teeth and then quite deliberately backed away. When my husband had been stretched as far as was possible. without actual injury, the donkey stopped. There she stood with a sort of smile on her face and the tie still between her teeth. After a minute or two she allowed her victim to go. When strangers are in the field engrossed with any donkey but her, she will get behind women members of the party, and put her nose under their coats or skirts and then raise it sharply; she will do this repeatedly unless notice is taken of her, quite plainly appreciating the squeaks of dismay. With men she simply butts from behind, quite gently but with insistence. MeMoke always spots a gate which has been left open, can stretch her neck right over any fence to sample some garden shrub which had been considered quite out of reach, appropriates the largest portion of hay, etc! Despite all this she is a steadying influence on the small herd, never losing her head, for instance, if some hysterical dog gets into the field and starts chasing — in fact he will soon find himself the one chased. The others look to her as the leader, and she has a reputation to keep up.

One of our most lovable donkeys is Mavourneen. She is not so "classy" as some of the others, but is so wonderful with children that she has had to be kept among the select breeding herd — as one breeds for temperament as well as for looks. The only trouble with Mavourneen is that if a fuss isn't made of her regularly, she sulks and will stand with her ears flat out on each side of her head if she feels neglected or too much attention is paid to another. She is photographed with a little girl at page 65.

This Jenny's rival with children is a young pure white Jenny, who equally cannot bear to be passed over by them. Because of her unusual appearance, they often do choose her for preference, to Mavourneen's discomfiture, and she follows visitors with small children about persistently until one of them is put on her back.

We have only owned one donkey that seemed to have no sense of fun at all, and she was old and bore the marks of hard treatment. Jenny was "not amused" by anything, and gave her foals an excellent but very strict upbringing — never hesitating to give them a hard nip if they became too rumbustious.

Donkeys make very deep friendships with each other and sometimes with ponies or horses. The particularly nervous Jenny mentioned in

Chapter 12 was watched over and faithfully guarded for some time by an aged grey pony until he had to be taken to another field. Both had been bought at the same horse fair from different owners and can never have met before — the donkey, who was about a year old, belonging to a batch that had come from Ireland. They travelled together in the same horse box to our home and were inseparable until the little donkey got used to new donkey friends and the pony went off to live with a horse.

The friendship can be between more than two. We have, for instance, what is known as "the Gang". This consists of four donkeys — the stallion and three young Jennies. They are always to be seen together whether sheltering or grazing, and join forces in trying to establish rights over as much of whatever kind of food is going as possible. On one occasion, when being transferred from one field to another by means of droving, which happens not infrequently, the Gang made a bid for freedom and bolted off into the woodland which surrounds our home. Having got the rest of the herd safely into the field, I spent the rest of the afternoon searching for them without success. We were considerably worried, as the wood abounds in yew trees. The following morning a friend, who is skilled in woodcraft, set off on a tracking expedition. He did eventually run the donkeys down a mile or so away at the entrance to our local prep school, where they would presumably have had a warm reception. They all looked thoroughly smug and were most unwilling to turn their steps in the direction of home. As their conductor had taken only one halter, the return journey proved very trying and only their refusal to be parted made it possible.

The humourless Jenny, mentioned above, was the only donkey we have had who appeared not to mind being alone. When without a foal, you would find her standing dreaming by herself, doing nothing in particular by the hour. I must add that she is now retired and has gone to live with two kind ladies who heap her with all the comforts a donkey could want on earth.

CHAPTER SIXTEEN

Your own donkey—a summary

You have bought your donkey, arranged for its transport, and now it has been safely delivered to your home. Most donkeys take travelling quite placidly and will walk down the ramp from the horsebox without fear, but full of curiosity as to their new surroundings. If you have children, restrain them if you can from rushing out with shrieks and yells of delight, and get them to greet their new pet quietly. If he shows signs of nervousness, hold him firmly by the halter in case he bolts for it, feed him some titbits, talk to him and stroke him. Keep the children from standing behind him and let him see them clearly as they come up to pat him. Then lead him into his paddock and un-halter him. He will probably immediately set off to explore his home and indulge in a good roll. You will already have seen that there is a supply of fresh water available and bedding in his stall. It may be kind to let him settle down for a day before the children start to ride, but this must, of course, be left to your own discretion. After he has been in the paddock for a little time, go in and give him a small mash, just so that he knows you are a friend; if it is winter, then you could simply take him his hay ration.

If you own dogs, it may be as well to let the donkey get used to its new home before introducing them, as, unless familiar with dogs, some donkeys will chase them. However, most dogs can keep out of the way well enough, and they usually make friends in the end — photograph at page 64. Our Golden Retriever was seen to climb on top of two of our more stolid donkeys when they were taking their ease lying down; she did it in the course of searching for some object she was sup-posed to retrieve, and the donkeys scarcely batted an eyelid.

On the first night pay a visit to the donkey before you go to bed to see that he has settled down, and perhaps give him a little extra hay or something to nibble.

The next day, if he is intended for riding,

try on his bridle and see whether he accepts the bit without fuss (see Chapter 9). If he is not going to be ridden bareback, put on the saddle and then teach the children — if they are old enough — how to saddle and bridle for themselves. (It is important that they learn correctly, because a twisted girth or strap can be painful and cause a sore). If the children are going to handle the bridling, etc., themselves, watch them for a few days until you are certain they have got it right. When they mount for the first time, hold on to the donkey's head if you are not sure about his antecedents, and walk him about for a few minutes to see whether he is quiet. I think one can say that almost invariably a Jenny or gelding is gentle and well-mannered, even if nervous on first arrival.

It is always as well to have a new animal looked over by the vet, so ask him to come and give a check-up and any advice he thinks necessary. Consult him about a worm powder and administer the first dose of this as soon as possible (Chapter 8), but remember not to exercise the donkey over much for the next day or two.

You will probably already have made contact with your local blacksmith, so if the donkey's hooves need attention, make an appointment with him to come as soon as he can arrange it.

Start calling the donkey by his name at once. He will learn it very quickly and in no time should be coming to the gate when called — usually it must be admitted, in the expectation of getting some edible delicacy.

I will end the chapter and the book by emphasising again the friendliness of a donkey. He will very soon become almost as much a member of the family as your dog. Remember that he is very sociable, and if he is living on his own in the paddock, give him plenty of attention. Braying usually means loneliness unless he is telling you that you are late with his breakfast on a cold winter morning. He is most intelligent, and you will find that he develops characteristics strictly his own, providing a great deal of fun for those of riper years as well as for the children. You may never quite know which of you has the upper hand, but although his mind is his own, he is patient, kind and not too demanding. So after all — who cares?

INDEX